# All About Colosseum: A Kid's Guide to Ancient Rome's Greatest Arena

**Educational Books For Kids, Volume 10**

Shah Rukh

Published by Shah Rukh, 2024.

ALL ABOUT COLOSSEUM: A KID'S GUIDE TO ANCIENT ROME'S GREATEST ARENA

**First edition. September 20, 2024.**

Copyright © 2024 Shah Rukh.

ISBN: 979-8227826237

Written by Shah Rukh.

# Table of Contents

# Prologue

Imagine a place where roaring crowds gathered to watch epic battles, where gladiators fought for their lives, and where wild beasts from distant lands roamed the arena. Welcome to the Colosseum, the greatest arena of Ancient Rome!

Over 2,000 years ago, the Colosseum stood as a symbol of the power and glory of the Roman Empire. It was more than just a stadium; it was a place where history was made, where stories of bravery, excitement, and adventure were lived out in front of thousands of spectators. This incredible structure, built from stone and imagination, has witnessed events that have shaped the course of history.

But the Colosseum is more than just an ancient ruin. It's a time machine that transports us back to a world of emperors and warriors, architects and engineers, wild animals and fearless fighters. In this book, you'll embark on a journey through time to explore the fascinating history, the incredible stories, and the amazing people who made the Colosseum the wonder it is today.

So, get ready to step into the shoes of a Roman spectator, a fearless gladiator, or even an emperor! As we explore the Colosseum together, you'll discover the secrets hidden within its walls, the legends that have been passed down through the centuries, and the lasting legacy of one of the greatest monuments in human history.

Are you ready to uncover the wonders of Ancient Rome's greatest arena? Let's begin our adventure!

# Chapter 1: The Grand Design of the Colosseum

The Colosseum stands as one of the most iconic architectural marvels of ancient Rome, a testament to the ingenuity and grandeur of Roman engineering. Its design was not only remarkable for its time but continues to impress people today with its sheer scale and complexity. Constructed between 70 and 80 AD under the emperors Vespasian and his son Titus, the Colosseum was primarily built as an arena for public spectacles, gladiatorial contests, and other forms of entertainment that could accommodate tens of thousands of spectators. To comprehend the full scope of its grand design, one must explore the materials used, the innovative techniques employed by Roman architects, and the sophisticated systems integrated into the building to manage the vast crowds that would flock to witness the events held within its walls.

The first thing that strikes people when they see the Colosseum is its immense size. It spans an area of about six acres, measuring approximately 620 feet in length and 513 feet in width, with a height reaching around 157 feet. The oval shape of the Colosseum was carefully chosen to ensure that everyone in the audience had a clear view of the central arena, no matter where they were seated. This design also helped the structure withstand the forces of the large crowds and any potential natural disasters, such as earthquakes, which have plagued the region over centuries. The outer wall was constructed using travertine limestone, a sturdy material that was quarried just outside Rome. Marble and tuff, a volcanic stone, were also used in the construction, each chosen for its specific properties to contribute to the stability and durability of the structure.

The design of the Colosseum's exterior was a triumph of Roman architecture. The building is made up of four levels, with each level displaying a different architectural order. The ground floor featured Tuscan columns, the second Ionic, and the third Corinthian, with the fourth floor displaying Corinthian pilasters. This mix of architectural styles was not merely decorative but symbolized the layers of society, as each style was considered more refined and elegant than the one below it. Arches formed a significant part of the Colosseum's design, both for aesthetic purposes and for structural support. There were 80 arched entrances on the ground level alone, allowing for the efficient flow of spectators in and out of the amphitheater. This was especially important because the Colosseum could hold up to 50,000 to 80,000 spectators, and managing such a massive crowd required thoughtful planning. These arches also provided natural light and ventilation, making the experience more comfortable for those attending the events.

One of the most impressive aspects of the Colosseum's design was its use of concrete. The Romans were pioneers in the use of concrete as a building material, and they perfected the formula to create a substance that was strong, versatile, and relatively inexpensive. The use of concrete allowed the architects to build the complex system of vaults and arches that supported the massive structure. These vaults distributed the weight of the building evenly, preventing any part of it from collapsing under its own weight. The inner walls of the Colosseum, which separated the different seating sections, were also built with concrete, providing the necessary support to hold up the upper levels of seating.

Inside the Colosseum, the design was equally impressive. The seating arrangements were a reflection of the hierarchical nature of Roman society. The emperor and other high-ranking officials had the best seats, closest to the action, while the general public sat farther away. There were specific sections designated for different classes of people, from senators to soldiers, to ordinary citizens, and even slaves. Women, unless they were part of the nobility, had to sit in the uppermost tiers. The arena itself, at the center of the Colosseum, was a masterpiece of design. It was covered with sand to absorb the blood from the battles and events that took place there. Beneath the arena floor was a complex network of tunnels and chambers, known as the hypogeum. This subterranean area housed the gladiators, animals, and machinery used to lift them into the arena. It also featured trapdoors and elevators that added an element of surprise to the games, allowing for dramatic entrances and sudden changes in the action.

The hypogeum, with its intricate system of passageways and rooms, was an engineering marvel in its own right. It allowed the organizers of the games to move animals and gladiators around without the audience seeing them until the moment they appeared in the arena. This system also ensured the safety of the performers and animals, preventing them from coming into contact with the spectators. The hypogeum was connected to various animal pens and armories, where the beasts and fighters were prepared before being released into the arena. There were also large elevators operated by pulleys and levers, which could quickly bring animals or people up to the surface, adding to the spectacle.

The Colosseum's sophisticated design didn't stop at its structural elements. The Romans also incorporated ingenious systems to manage the large crowds that attended events. The vomitoria, a series of passageways and staircases, allowed the spectators to enter and exit the amphitheater quickly and efficiently. These passageways were designed to prevent overcrowding and bottlenecks, ensuring that the audience could leave the building in a matter of minutes. The Colosseum also had a retractable awning system known as the velarium. This massive canvas canopy was operated by sailors from the Roman navy, who would unfurl it over the seating areas to provide shade for the spectators on hot days. The velarium was an essential feature in a city as sunny as Rome, and its operation required a high degree of coordination and expertise.

Another remarkable feature of the Colosseum's design was its adaptability. While it was primarily built for gladiatorial contests, the arena could also be flooded for mock naval battles, known as naumachiae. This required a complex system of aqueducts and drains to bring water into the arena and then remove it afterward. The fact that the Colosseum could be transformed from a battleground for gladiators to a stage for naval warfare speaks to the flexibility of its design. Over the centuries, the Colosseum has withstood earthquakes, fires, and even neglect. Despite the damage it has sustained, including the loss of much of its outer wall, it remains an iconic symbol of the grandeur of ancient Rome.

The grand design of the Colosseum is a reflection of the power and ambition of the Roman Empire. It was a statement to the world that Rome was capable of building something unparalleled in size, complexity, and functionality. Every detail, from the arrangement of the seats to the engineering of the arches, was carefully considered to ensure that the Colosseum would not only serve as an entertainment venue but also stand as a lasting monument to Roman innovation. Its enduring presence serves as a reminder of the incredible achievements of ancient Roman architects and engineers, whose work continues to inspire and astonish to this day. The Colosseum was not just a building; it was a symbol of the empire's ability to conquer not only lands but also the challenges of design and construction, creating a space that could bring together thousands of people to witness the might and splendor of Rome.

# Chapter 2: A Day at the Roman Games

A day at the Roman games was a spectacle like no other, filled with excitement, anticipation, and the roar of tens of thousands of spectators packed into the towering walls of the Colosseum. For the citizens of Rome, attending the games was not just an opportunity to watch thrilling battles and daring feats, but also a social event, a chance to mingle with people from all walks of life, from the emperor and senators to the common folk. The games themselves were a reflection of the might, wealth, and influence of the Roman Empire, showcasing not only the strength of its gladiators and the exotic animals brought from the far corners of the empire, but also the elaborate and well-orchestrated events that were held with precise timing and grand scale.

The day would begin early, often at dawn, as the spectators arrived to claim their seats in the Colosseum. With a seating capacity of between 50,000 and 80,000, the amphitheater was designed to accommodate vast numbers of people, and the crowd was made up of a cross-section of Roman society. The best seats, close to the arena, were reserved for the emperor, senators, and other high-ranking officials, while the common citizens, soldiers, and even slaves filled the higher tiers. There were strict seating arrangements based on social status, with the emperor's box offering a perfect view of the entire arena, while the lowest tiers were often reserved for women and the lower classes. The crowd would be buzzing with excitement, eager to witness the day's events, as food and drink vendors made their way through the aisles, selling bread, fruits, and wine to the spectators who had come to spend the entire day at the games.

The Roman games were divided into different segments, each designed to entertain and enthrall the audience. The day often began with displays of wild animals, which had been brought to Rome from across the empire, showcasing the power and reach of Roman influence. These animals, including lions, tigers, elephants, and bears, would be paraded around the arena before being pitted against each other or against trained hunters known as bestiarii. The sight of these exotic beasts was intended to impress the crowd, as many Romans would have never seen such animals before. The hunters, armed with spears, swords, and nets, would demonstrate their bravery and skill as they fought the dangerous creatures, often to the death. The audience would cheer or gasp, depending on the outcome, as the animals were slain, and the hunters either emerged victorious or fell prey to the ferocity of their opponents.

After the animal hunts, there would often be a short intermission, during which the arena was prepared for the next stage of the games. This might involve cleaning the sand to remove the blood and remains of the animals, or adjusting the scenery if there were to be any staged battles or mock naval engagements later in the day. During these breaks, entertainers would sometimes perform to keep the crowd engaged. Jugglers, acrobats, and musicians might fill the arena, performing feats of dexterity and skill while the audience relaxed and refreshed themselves.

The midday segment of the games was often the most brutal and gory, known as the execution of criminals or prisoners. These unfortunate individuals, often condemned to death for their crimes, were sent into the arena with little chance of survival. They might be forced to fight each other to the death, or be given basic weapons to face off against trained gladiators or wild animals. Sometimes the executions were carried out in particularly creative or theatrical ways, designed to entertain the audience as much as to punish the condemned. The Colosseum's arena floor, which was covered in sand to absorb the blood, would become a stage for death, with the crowd cheering or jeering as the prisoners met their fate. For the Romans, this was a stark reminder of the power of the empire and its ability to dispense justice, however harsh.

The main event of the day, and the part that the crowd looked forward to the most, was the gladiatorial combat. Gladiators were often slaves, prisoners of war, or criminals who had been trained in special schools to fight in the arena. However, some gladiators were free men who had volunteered for the role, seeking fame, fortune, or simply the thrill of battle. The life of a gladiator was dangerous, and while many died in the arena, those who survived could gain considerable fame and adulation from the Roman public. Gladiators were trained to fight in specific styles, each with their own distinctive weapons and armor. For example, the heavily armored murmillo fought with a sword and large shield, while the lightly armed retiarius wielded a trident and net, using his agility to outmaneuver his opponents.

The gladiatorial combats were carefully orchestrated to provide maximum entertainment for the audience. The fights were not simply chaotic brawls; they were often pitched as contests of skill and strategy, with the crowd fully invested in the outcome. Some gladiators became famous, and the crowd would shout their names, offering support or calling for their defeat. The fate of a losing gladiator was sometimes left to the decision of the emperor or the crowd, who could either spare the fighter's life or signal for his execution by raising their thumbs. The drama of these moments was intense, as a gladiator knelt before the emperor, awaiting his decision, while the crowd's collective voice rose in either mercy or bloodlust. If the gladiator was spared, he might live to fight another day and perhaps even win his freedom through continued victories. However, if the emperor or the crowd chose death, the gladiator would meet his end in the sand of the arena, a final sacrifice to the entertainment of Rome.

The conclusion of the day might feature a grand spectacle, such as a reenactment of a famous battle or a naval engagement. The Colosseum was equipped with systems that allowed it to be flooded, turning the arena into a vast pool where ships could be launched and mock sea battles, known as naumachiae, could be staged. These events required extensive preparation, as the ships had to be constructed and the water brought in through aqueducts. The battles themselves, while staged, were often still dangerous for the participants, many of whom were prisoners or slaves forced to fight. The sight of ships clashing, men struggling in the water, and the sounds of battle would have filled the Colosseum with excitement as the crowd watched the dramatic recreation of Rome's military victories. Even though these events were highly controlled, there was always an element of unpredictability that thrilled the audience.

Throughout the day, the atmosphere in the Colosseum would have been electric. The noise of the crowd, the spectacle of blood and bravery, and the sense of being part of something larger than life made attending the games an unforgettable experience. For the citizens of Rome, the games were more than just entertainment; they were a symbol of the empire's power and the emperor's generosity. By providing free games, the emperor kept the people happy and distracted from political concerns, using the Colosseum as a tool of social control. The games were a demonstration of Roman superiority, not only in terms of military might but also in the mastery of architecture, engineering, and public spectacle. For the spectators, a day at the Roman games was a thrilling escape from their daily lives, an opportunity to witness feats of courage, skill, and strength in a setting that was both awe-inspiring and terrifying.

As the day drew to a close, the crowd would begin to filter out of the Colosseum, still buzzing with the excitement of what they had witnessed. Some would discuss the day's events with their neighbors, debating the bravery of the gladiators or the outcome of a particularly intense fight. Others would head to nearby taverns or bathhouses, continuing the social aspect of the day in the company of friends or fellow citizens. For many, the games were not just about the spectacle itself but about the experience of being part of something grand, something that tied them to the power and majesty of Rome. And as the sun set over the city, the Colosseum would stand as a towering reminder of the empire's glory, its walls echoing with the cheers and cries of the thousands who had filled its seats, eager to witness the awe-inspiring events of a day at the Roman games.

# Chapter 3: The Mighty Gladiators of Rome

The mighty gladiators of Rome were some of the most iconic and enduring figures of the ancient world. Their blood-soaked battles and larger-than-life personas captivated audiences and became a central part of Roman culture, especially during the height of the Roman Empire. These fighters were more than just men thrown into the arena to meet their fate; they were symbols of strength, bravery, and sometimes defiance. For many, the life of a gladiator was one of harsh realities, marked by physical exhaustion, constant danger, and the ever-present specter of death. Yet, for others, it offered a path to fame, fortune, and even freedom.

The tradition of gladiatorial combat began as a form of funeral ritual, believed to have originated with the Etruscans, an ancient civilization in Italy. These early contests were meant to honor the dead, with prisoners or slaves fighting to the death as a form of sacrifice. However, as Rome expanded and its culture grew more sophisticated, the practice evolved into a form of public entertainment. By the time of the Roman Republic and later the Roman Empire, gladiatorial games had become a highly organized and state-sponsored spectacle, drawing massive crowds to amphitheaters like the Colosseum. While the origin of the term "gladiator" comes from the Latin word "gladius," meaning sword, not all gladiators wielded this weapon. They were trained in various fighting styles, each with its own unique equipment and combat strategies.

Gladiators came from a variety of backgrounds. The majority were slaves, prisoners of war, or criminals condemned to fight as punishment for their crimes. For these men, the life of a gladiator was often brutal and short, with little hope of escape. Yet, despite their lowly status, gladiators could rise to become some of the most famous figures in

Roman society, admired by the public for their skill and courage. Some gladiators were free men who volunteered for the role, often motivated by the promise of wealth and glory. These volunteers, known as "auctorati," willingly signed contracts to fight in the arena, even though they risked injury or death. For some, the chance to win fame or secure a better life for themselves or their families outweighed the dangers they faced in the arena.

The training of gladiators was a rigorous and disciplined process, overseen by professional trainers at special schools known as "ludi." These schools were often run by wealthy businessmen who invested in the gladiators and sought to profit from their victories in the arena. The training regimen was harsh and physically demanding, with gladiators practicing their combat skills daily, honing their bodies for the trials they would face in the arena. They were trained to fight in specific styles, each with its own set of weapons, armor, and tactics. Some of the most well-known types of gladiators included the murmillo, who fought with a large shield and short sword; the thraex, who wielded a curved sword and fought with a small shield; and the retiarius, who fought with a trident and net, relying on agility and speed to defeat heavily armored opponents.

The life of a gladiator was often one of isolation. Though they trained and lived together in their schools, the men were rivals, constantly aware that one day they might be called upon to fight each other in the arena. Outside of their schools, gladiators were typically separated from the rest of Roman society. Though they were admired for their bravery, they were also considered outcasts, especially those who had been slaves or criminals. Despite this, some gladiators managed to achieve a level of fame that transcended their status. Victorious gladiators were celebrated by the public and sometimes lavished with gifts by wealthy patrons. Those who fought with exceptional skill or bravery could become popular heroes, with the Roman people chanting their names during games and even requesting their image on frescoes or pottery. These gladiators enjoyed a level of celebrity that offered them privileges and wealth, despite the inherent dangers of their profession.

While many gladiators faced bleak prospects, there was a potential reward for those who survived long enough to achieve glory in the arena. Gladiators who won numerous battles and demonstrated their prowess could be awarded a wooden sword called a "rudis." This symbolized their freedom, and a gladiator who received it was no longer bound to fight. Though rare, some former gladiators went on to live prosperous lives, using the fame and wealth they had earned in the arena to secure their futures. Others remained connected to the world of gladiators, either as trainers or in other roles within the gladiatorial games.

For many, however, the life of a gladiator was a short and brutal one. Injuries were common, and death was a constant threat. While not every fight was to the death, many were, and even in those that weren't, a serious injury could mean the end of a gladiator's career. Gladiators often had short lifespans, especially those who were forced into the role as slaves or criminals. The allure of freedom or fame may have driven some to embrace the life of a gladiator, but for many, it was simply a means of survival in a world where their choices were limited.

The actual gladiatorial combat in the arena was a highly structured affair, more akin to a theatrical performance than the chaotic battles one might imagine. Each match was carefully choreographed to provide maximum entertainment for the crowd. Gladiators were paired based on their fighting styles, with the goal of creating a balance between strength and agility, or defense and offense. The audience was always a central part of the spectacle, with their reactions and cheers influencing the dynamics of the fight. A skilled gladiator not only had to be a master of combat but also needed to play to the crowd, winning their favor by showing off his bravery, technique, and endurance. The relationship between the gladiator and the crowd was a key part of the games, and many gladiators became experts at manipulating the emotions of the spectators, using their skill and charisma to turn even a losing battle into a heroic struggle.

The outcome of a gladiatorial fight was not always determined by death. In many cases, a losing gladiator would fall to the ground, and his fate would be left in the hands of the editor of the games, often the emperor or another high-ranking official, as well as the crowd. If the defeated gladiator had fought bravely, the crowd might call for his life to be spared by waving handkerchiefs or giving the thumbs up. Conversely, if the gladiator had performed poorly or the crowd desired more bloodshed, they could call for his execution with a thumbs down gesture. The final decision rested with the editor, but public opinion often swayed the outcome. For the gladiator, this moment was a crucial one, and the suspense added to the drama of the games.

The death of a gladiator, though not always the intended outcome, was a regular feature of the games. The bloodshed, while horrific by modern standards, was a key aspect of the entertainment for Roman audiences. The spectacle of violence, the thrill of life-and-death struggles, and the display of courage in the face of death were all part of what made the games so captivating. For the Roman people, the arena was a place where the values of the empire—strength, bravery, and the power of life over death—were put on display in a way that was both horrifying and exhilarating.

The legacy of the gladiators has endured for centuries, long after the fall of the Roman Empire. Their stories, both real and mythologized, continue to capture the imagination. From ancient Roman texts to modern films and literature, the gladiators have come to symbolize the complex interplay between power, entertainment, and human resilience. Though they were often victims of a brutal and unforgiving system, many gladiators achieved a kind of immortality through their feats in the arena. Their battles, once fought for the amusement of a

Roman audience, are now remembered as a testament to the strength of the human spirit in the face of overwhelming odds.

The mighty gladiators of Rome, whether they fought for freedom, fame, or mere survival, played a crucial role in the culture of the Roman Empire. Their lives were marked by both tragedy and triumph, pain and glory. In the sands of the Colosseum and other arenas, they faced impossible challenges, and though many fell, those who rose to greatness did so with the eyes of an empire upon them. The gladiators were not only warriors; they were performers, symbols, and, in some cases, legends whose stories continue to be told, long after the last sword was drawn.

# Chapter 4: Secrets of the Colosseum's Underground

Beneath the towering arches and grand stone façade of the Colosseum, hidden from the eyes of the roaring crowds, lay a vast and complex subterranean world that was essential to the spectacular shows and brutal combats that unfolded in the arena above. Known as the "hypogeum," this intricate network of underground chambers, tunnels, and passageways was a feat of engineering genius and a marvel of Roman architectural innovation. It was here, deep beneath the sandy arena floor, that much of the preparation for the games took place, and where the true secrets of the Colosseum's grandeur were held.

The hypogeum was not part of the original design of the Colosseum when construction began under Emperor Vespasian in AD 70. The underground complex was added later during the reign of Emperor Domitian, Vespasian's son, in an effort to enhance the spectacle and functionality of the games. Before the construction of the hypogeum, the Colosseum's arena could be flooded to host mock naval battles, known as "naumachiae," in which ships would engage in dramatic combat for the entertainment of the crowds. However, once the hypogeum was built, these battles ceased, as the underground structure took up the space beneath the arena floor. In exchange, the Romans gained a far more versatile and dynamic system for staging all kinds of events, including gladiatorial contests, animal hunts, and elaborate executions.

The hypogeum itself was a two-level network of tunnels, rooms, and cages, all meticulously designed to support the performances taking place above. It was here that gladiators, animals, and stage props were housed before being lifted into the arena through a system of elevators, ramps, and trapdoors. The complexity of this underground world allowed for an almost seamless flow of action in the arena. As spectators watched in awe, they were often unaware of the careful coordination taking place beneath their feet, as fighters and animals were prepared, and elaborate scenery was set for the next act of the games.

One of the most remarkable features of the hypogeum was the system of elevators and trapdoors that allowed for dramatic entrances and sudden appearances in the arena. These devices were operated by a team of slaves and workers, who used pulleys, winches, and counterweights to raise and lower platforms through the arena floor. There were an estimated 80 vertical shafts throughout the hypogeum, each one leading to a trapdoor above. Some of these trapdoors were large enough to allow entire sets of scenery or groups of animals to emerge from below, while others were designed for individual gladiators or beasts to make their entrance. The timing of these appearances had to be precise to maintain the flow of the spectacle above, and the workers in the hypogeum were responsible for ensuring that everything went off without a hitch.

In addition to the elevators and trapdoors, the hypogeum housed numerous cages and holding areas for the animals that would participate in the games. These creatures were often exotic and dangerous, brought to Rome from distant lands as a demonstration of the empire's power and reach. Lions, tigers, bears, elephants, and even crocodiles were kept in the underground chambers, where they would be starved or agitated before being released into the arena to fight against hunters, known as "bestiarii," or to battle one another in savage displays of nature's most fearsome predators. The animals were kept in darkness, which heightened their ferocity when they were suddenly thrust into the blinding light of the arena. For the audience, the sight of a lion or a tiger emerging from beneath the floor, seemingly out of nowhere, added an element of surprise and excitement to the games.

The hypogeum was also home to the gladiators before their matches. While some gladiators waited in barracks or holding cells above ground, others were kept below, hidden from the audience until it was their time to fight. The tension in the air must have been palpable as these men, many of whom were slaves or prisoners of war, prepared themselves for combat, knowing that their fate would soon be decided by the sword. They would likely have heard the roars of the crowd above, a constant reminder of the life-or-death battle they were about to face. For some, the hypogeum was a place of final preparation, where they steeled themselves for the fight ahead. For others, it was a kind of purgatory, a waiting area before the ultimate judgment in the arena.

The workers and slaves who operated the hypogeum were crucial to the success of the games. These individuals, often overlooked in the grand spectacle of the Colosseum, were responsible for maintaining the flow of events. They worked tirelessly in the dark, cramped conditions of the underground chambers, moving animals into place, managing the gladiators, and ensuring that the intricate system of elevators and trapdoors functioned smoothly. Without their efforts, the seamless transition between acts in the arena would not have been possible. Their work was dangerous, especially when dealing with wild animals, and there was always the risk of accidents or malfunctions. The hypogeum, while hidden from the public eye, was an essential part of the Colosseum's spectacle, and those who labored within it played a critical role in bringing the games to life.

One of the lesser-known aspects of the hypogeum was its use as a staging area for executions. In addition to gladiatorial combat and animal hunts, the Colosseum hosted public executions of criminals, prisoners of war, and those condemned for various offenses. These executions were often designed to be as theatrical as possible, with the condemned being forced to fight wild animals or being subjected to elaborate and cruel punishments. The hypogeum was where these individuals would spend their final moments before being led into the arena to face their fate. In some cases, elaborate sets were constructed underground and then raised into the arena, transforming the space into a battlefield, a mythological scene, or even a re-creation of a famous Roman victory. The condemned might be dressed as characters from mythology or history, with their deaths meant to mimic the fall of an enemy of Rome or the punishment of a figure from legend. These executions were not merely about justice; they were designed to entertain, to shock, and to reaffirm the power of the empire.

The hypogeum, while hidden from the view of the spectators, was a place of constant activity. The sounds of chains clanking, animals growling, and the creaking of wooden platforms echoed through the tunnels as workers rushed to ensure that the games proceeded without interruption. The atmosphere below was likely tense, filled with the smell of animals and sweat, as men and beasts alike prepared for their moment in the spotlight. The underground chambers also had a darker side, as they were often a place of fear and suffering for the condemned. While the Colosseum's audience reveled in the excitement and drama above, the hypogeum was a world of preparation, anticipation, and sometimes despair.

The engineering of the hypogeum was a testament to the Romans' mastery of construction and design. It was carefully planned to maximize efficiency and ensure that the flow of events in the arena above remained continuous and seamless. The tunnels and passageways were laid out in a way that allowed workers to move quickly between different parts of the hypogeum, and the elevators and trapdoors were designed to operate smoothly despite the massive weights they often carried. The Romans' ability to build such a complex underground system, while also ensuring that the Colosseum above remained a stable and grand structure, speaks to their advanced knowledge of architecture and engineering.

Despite its importance to the games, the hypogeum remained a hidden part of the Colosseum for centuries. It was only in more recent times, through archaeological excavations and research, that the full extent of the underground structure was revealed. Today, visitors to the Colosseum can explore parts of the hypogeum, gaining a deeper understanding of the incredible complexity that lay beneath the arena floor. Walking through the narrow tunnels and chambers, one can almost imagine the sights and sounds that once filled this underground world—the clattering of weapons, the snarls of animals, and the whispered conversations of gladiators preparing for battle.

The secrets of the Colosseum's underground reveal just how carefully orchestrated and meticulously planned the Roman games were. Far from being mere spectacles of violence, the games were a highly organized form of entertainment, designed to keep the audience engaged from start to finish. The hypogeum was the engine that made it all possible, hidden away from the public's view but essential to the grandeur and excitement of the Colosseum. This underground world of tunnels, cages, and machinery was a place of both precision and danger, a testament to Roman ingenuity and a reminder of the darker side of the empire's entertainment. While the crowds above cheered for their favorite gladiators and marveled at the exotic animals that appeared before them, the real work of the Colosseum was taking place beneath their feet, in the shadows of the hypogeum, where the secrets of Rome's greatest arena lay hidden, waiting to be revealed.

# Chapter 5: Wild Beasts in the Arena

In the grand spectacle of the Roman Colosseum, few elements captured the imagination of the audience quite like the appearance of wild beasts in the arena. These animals, often exotic and fearsome, were brought from the farthest reaches of the Roman Empire to participate in the dramatic and often brutal games that entertained the citizens of Rome. Known as *venationes*—animal hunts—these events were a regular part of the Colosseum's program and played a central role in reinforcing the power, wealth, and reach of the empire. The inclusion of wild beasts in the games served as a testament to Rome's dominion over nature and its ability to control even the most dangerous and majestic creatures on Earth.

The animals used in these events were varied and diverse, hailing from distant lands that Rome had conquered or established trade with. Lions, tigers, leopards, bears, elephants, rhinos, hippos, and even crocodiles were among the many species that made their way to the Colosseum. Some animals were captured in the dense jungles of Africa, others in the forests of Europe or the plains of Asia. The sheer diversity of these creatures was meant to astound the audience, many of whom would never have seen such animals in their lives. The Romans prided themselves on their ability to bring the wonders of the world to their city, and the presence of these wild beasts in the arena was a vivid demonstration of that power.

The process of capturing, transporting, and housing these animals was a massive undertaking that required an extensive network of hunters, traders, and slaves. Once an animal was captured, it had to be transported across vast distances, often by ship or cart, to the heart of the empire. This journey was long and perilous, with many animals dying along the way from the stress of captivity or the harsh conditions of travel. The ones that survived were kept in cages until they were ready to be released into the arena. The Romans built special facilities near the Colosseum to house these animals, ensuring that they were well-fed and ready for their role in the games. However, it was not uncommon for the animals to be starved or mistreated before being sent into the arena, as this would often make them more aggressive and dangerous when they finally faced the hunters or gladiators.

The *venationes* were often staged as elaborate hunts, with skilled fighters known as *bestiarii* tasked with battling the wild animals. These hunters were specially trained for the dangerous task of confronting the beasts, and they often fought with spears, swords, and nets. While some *bestiarii* were experienced professionals who could earn fame and fortune through their victories in the arena, others were criminals, slaves, or prisoners of war who were forced to fight as punishment. For these unfortunate individuals, the games often meant a brutal and bloody death. The fight between man and beast was meant to symbolize the dominance of humanity over nature, and the crowd cheered as the hunter's skill or the animal's ferocity was put on display.

In addition to the individual hunts, there were also large-scale battles involving dozens of animals at once. These grand spectacles were designed to be as impressive and awe-inspiring as possible, with entire forests or deserts recreated in the arena to provide a suitable backdrop for the action. Trees, rocks, and other scenery were lowered into the arena through the trapdoors in the hypogeum, transforming the space into a vivid representation of the animal's natural habitat. The sheer scale of these productions was meant to demonstrate the Roman's ability to recreate any part of the world within their great city, further reinforcing the empire's dominance over distant lands.

In some cases, the *venationes* involved multiple species of animals, pitting lions against tigers, bears against bulls, or even elephants against rhinoceroses. These battles were often unpredictable and could lead to dramatic moments of carnage as the animals tore into each other. The sight of two massive beasts locked in combat was a thrilling experience for the audience, who would watch in awe as blood soaked the sand of the arena floor. It was not uncommon for these events to end with the deaths of both animals, their bodies dragged away to make room for the next act. For the Romans, this was all part of the spectacle—an expression of nature's savagery, controlled and directed by the hands of the empire.

The use of animals in executions was another grim feature of the Colosseum's wild beast spectacles. Condemned criminals and prisoners, often those sentenced for treason or serious crimes, were sometimes thrown into the arena to be devoured by lions, tigers, or other dangerous creatures. This form of execution, known as *damnatio ad bestias* (condemnation to the beasts), was not just a method of punishment; it was also designed as a public spectacle, a way to entertain the masses while simultaneously serving as a warning to others who might think of defying Roman law. The prisoners were often unarmed or given only rudimentary weapons, making their survival all but impossible. The crowd reveled in the terror and brutality of the spectacle, watching as the condemned tried in vain to defend themselves against the oncoming onslaught of claws and teeth. These public executions were an especially gruesome part of the Roman games, blending entertainment with punishment in a way that demonstrated the empire's willingness to use violence to maintain control.

Perhaps one of the most dramatic uses of wild animals in the Colosseum was during the staging of mythological or historical reenactments. The Romans had a particular love for dramatizing famous legends, and the arena often served as a stage for these stories. For example, the myth of Orpheus, who was torn apart by wild beasts, could be reenacted in the Colosseum, with a criminal playing the role of Orpheus and being subjected to a similar fate. In another famous example, the Colosseum was used to recreate the labors of Hercules, with the hero battling lions, bulls, and other creatures. These mythological displays were designed not only to entertain but to connect the Roman games to the broader cultural and religious traditions of the empire. By incorporating these legends into the spectacle of the arena, the Romans were able to merge their fascination with the divine and the brutal reality of the games, creating a spectacle that appealed to both the spiritual and violent sensibilities of the audience.

The presence of wild beasts in the Colosseum was not merely about entertainment; it was also a powerful political tool. The *venationes* were often held to commemorate military victories, with the animals symbolizing the peoples and lands conquered by Rome. By bringing these exotic creatures into the arena, the emperors could demonstrate the vastness of the empire and its ability to command the resources of the world. The animals, like the conquered peoples they represented, were subdued and controlled by Roman might. In this way, the games became a celebration of imperial power, a way for the emperors to reinforce their authority and remind the citizens of Rome's greatness.

The emperors themselves sometimes played a direct role in the wild beast hunts, either by overseeing the events or even participating in the battles. Emperor Commodus, for example, is known to have fought in the arena against wild animals, although his participation was largely symbolic, with the fights carefully staged to ensure his safety. Nonetheless, the image of an emperor battling a lion or slaying an elephant would have been a powerful symbol of strength and dominance. For the audience, it was an opportunity to see their ruler as a hero, capable of conquering not only human enemies but also the forces of nature.

Despite the brutality of the animal hunts, the Romans viewed the *venationes* as a celebration of their mastery over the natural world. The ability to control and subdue wild beasts was seen as a reflection of Rome's power and civilization. For the spectators, the sight of a lion, tiger, or bear emerging from beneath the arena floor was both thrilling and terrifying—a reminder of the dangers that existed beyond the borders of the empire. But in the controlled environment of the Colosseum, those dangers were subdued, and the animals were little more than another element of the grand spectacle, their lives and deaths serving as entertainment for the masses.

Over the centuries, countless animals were killed in the Colosseum, and the toll on the natural world was immense. Some historians estimate that hundreds of thousands of animals may have been used in the games, leading to the depletion of certain species in the regions from which they were captured. Elephants, lions, and other large animals became increasingly rare as the demand for more and more exotic beasts grew. The *venationes* were not just a spectacle of human dominance over nature; they were also a destructive force that had a lasting impact on the environment and the wildlife of the ancient world.

As the Roman Empire began to decline, so too did the scale of the wild beast hunts. The resources needed to capture and transport the animals became harder to come by, and the empire's ability to project its power through the games waned. By the time the Colosseum ceased to be used for regular games in the early medieval period, the days of the grand *venationes* were long past. But the legacy of these events endured, and the image of the wild beasts in the arena remains one of the most enduring symbols of the Colosseum and the violent, spectacular world of the Roman games.

The use of wild beasts in the Colosseum was more than just a form of entertainment; it was a reflection of the empire's values, its power, and its relationship with the natural world. The *venationes* were a spectacle of life and death, of human civilization's attempt to tame the untamable. In the roar of the crowd and the blood-soaked sands of the arena, the wild beasts of the Roman Colosseum left an indelible mark on history, a testament to the grandeur, brutality, and complexity of the ancient world.

# Chapter 6: The Colosseum's Ingenious Engineering

The Colosseum stands as one of the most remarkable achievements of ancient Roman engineering, a testament to the ingenuity and architectural prowess of the empire at its height. Its construction, completed around 80 AD under the Emperor Titus, revolutionized the concept of public entertainment spaces and introduced several innovative techniques and structures that would influence architecture for centuries to come. To truly appreciate the magnitude of this engineering marvel, one must consider the many groundbreaking features incorporated into the Colosseum's design—its massive size, advanced use of materials, intricate structural systems, and the unique technological advancements that made the spectacles within its walls possible.

The sheer scale of the Colosseum was unlike anything that had come before it. Measuring approximately 189 meters long and 156 meters wide, with a height of about 50 meters, the arena could hold an estimated 50,000 to 80,000 spectators. Its oval shape ensured that every member of the audience, no matter where they were seated, had a clear view of the events unfolding in the center of the arena. The Romans meticulously planned the seating arrangements, dividing the space into different tiers based on social hierarchy. The wealthiest and most powerful citizens, such as senators and nobles, sat closest to the action, while commoners and slaves occupied the upper levels. Despite its size, the Colosseum's design allowed for quick and efficient movement of people. Its entrances and exits, known as *vomitoria*, were strategically placed to ensure that the arena could be filled or emptied in a matter of minutes—a remarkable feat, considering the number of people it could accommodate.

The construction of the Colosseum required an unprecedented amount of resources, labor, and material. Tens of thousands of slaves, prisoners of war, and skilled laborers worked tirelessly to complete the structure over a period of several years. The primary materials used in its construction were travertine limestone, tuff (a volcanic rock), and concrete—a relatively new invention at the time that would later revolutionize Roman building practices. Travertine, sourced from quarries outside Rome, was used for the outer walls and structural skeleton of the Colosseum, providing a strong and durable frame. Tuff and brick were used for the internal walls, while concrete, made by mixing lime and volcanic ash, was used to create the vaults and other complex structural elements. This use of concrete allowed the Romans to build larger and more intricate structures than ever before, as it could be poured into molds and shaped to fit the precise needs of the design. Concrete also dried quickly and was much lighter than stone, reducing the weight of the massive structure and preventing it from collapsing under its own size.

One of the most ingenious aspects of the Colosseum's engineering was its use of arches and vaults. The Romans perfected the use of the arch, which allowed them to distribute the weight of the structure evenly and support massive loads without the need for solid walls. The Colosseum's outer façade consists of a series of 80 arches on each level, forming a continuous colonnade that gives the building its iconic look. These arches not only provided structural support but also created open spaces for entrances and exits, as well as for decorative statues and inscriptions. Behind the outer arches, the internal structure of the Colosseum is made up of a complex system of barrel vaults and groin vaults—arched ceilings formed by intersecting two barrel vaults at right angles. These vaults helped to distribute the weight of the seating areas and created strong, open spaces for the corridors and staircases beneath the stands. The use of arches and vaults was crucial in enabling the Romans to build a structure as large and as durable as the

Colosseum, and this architectural innovation would go on to influence buildings throughout history.

The Colosseum's seating arrangement was another feat of engineering brilliance. The sloping stands were supported by a complex series of barrel vaults and buttresses, which allowed the Romans to build the seating areas high above the ground without sacrificing stability. The seats themselves were made of stone and arranged in tiers, with each row slightly higher than the one in front of it, ensuring that everyone had a clear view of the arena. The stands were divided into four main sections: the *podium, maenianum primum, maenianum secundum*, and *maenianum summum*, each reserved for different classes of society. The lowest section, the *podium*, was reserved for the emperor, senators, and other elite members of society, while the upper sections were for the general public. The very top of the Colosseum, the *summum maenianum in ligneis*, was a wooden platform reserved for women and the lowest classes. The design of the seating ensured that the Colosseum could accommodate tens of thousands of spectators, and the system of staircases, corridors, and entrances allowed for easy access and movement throughout the structure.

Another ingenious feature of the Colosseum was its retractable awning, known as the *velarium*. This massive canopy was designed to protect spectators from the sun and rain, allowing events to continue in a range of weather conditions. The *velarium* was supported by a series of wooden masts that were inserted into sockets at the top of the Colosseum's outer wall. These masts were connected by ropes to a system of pulleys, which allowed the awning to be drawn over the seating area when needed. Sailors from the Roman navy, skilled in the art of handling ropes and sails, were responsible for operating the *velarium*. The canopy itself was made of linen and could be adjusted to provide shade for different sections of the audience, depending on the position of the sun. The design and operation of the *velarium* were incredibly advanced for the time, and the ability to provide comfort for tens of thousands of spectators was a remarkable achievement in Roman engineering.

The Colosseum's floor, known as the *arena*, was another example of Roman ingenuity. The word "arena" comes from the Latin word for sand, which was used to cover the floor and absorb the blood and other fluids from the events. Beneath the sand, however, lay a complex network of chambers, tunnels, and passageways known as the *hypogeum*. The *hypogeum* was a two-level subterranean structure that housed gladiators, animals, and stage machinery. It contained a series of elevators and trapdoors that allowed gladiators and animals to be raised directly into the arena, creating dramatic entrances that thrilled the audience. The *hypogeum* also included storage rooms for props, as well as cells for holding condemned prisoners and dangerous animals. The ability to hide these elements beneath the floor of the Colosseum and then reveal them at the perfect moment added to the drama and spectacle of the games. The engineering of the *hypogeum* was so advanced that some historians compare it to modern-day stage machinery, and it played a crucial role in the success of the Colosseum's entertainment.

Water engineering was also a significant aspect of the Colosseum's design. While the Colosseum is best known for hosting gladiatorial combat and animal hunts, it was also used for naval battles, known as *naumachiae*, during the early years of its existence. To stage these mock sea battles, the Romans devised an ingenious system for flooding the arena. The floor of the Colosseum could be removed, and water could be channeled into the arena from nearby aqueducts. The water level could be controlled to create shallow or deep pools, depending on the requirements of the event. Small boats, built to replicate ships from famous battles, would then be brought into the arena, and the spectacle would unfold as gladiators or condemned prisoners fought to the death on these makeshift vessels. The ability to transform the arena into a water-filled battleground demonstrated the Romans' mastery of hydraulic engineering and added another layer of entertainment to the Colosseum's diverse program of events. However, as the need for larger and more elaborate spectacles grew, the naval battles were phased out, and the *hypogeum* was built, making it impossible to flood the arena any longer.

Beyond its physical structure, the Colosseum was a marvel of logistical engineering. Hosting events for tens of thousands of spectators required a sophisticated system for managing the crowds, providing amenities, and ensuring the safety and comfort of the audience. The Romans constructed a series of public restrooms, drinking fountains, and food stalls within the Colosseum, ensuring that spectators could remain in the arena for extended periods without leaving. The *vomitoria*—the entrances and exits—were designed to prevent bottlenecks and allow for the quick evacuation of the arena in case of emergencies. The entire structure was a carefully orchestrated machine, designed to handle the massive influx of people that gathered for the games. The fact that the Colosseum could host events without major incidents, despite the vast number of people in attendance, speaks to the incredible foresight and planning that went into its design.

In conclusion, the Colosseum was not only a symbol of Roman power and grandeur but also a testament to the empire's mastery of engineering and architecture. Its construction pushed the boundaries of what was possible at the time, incorporating innovative techniques and materials that would influence architecture for centuries to come. From its massive scale and intricate seating arrangements to its underground chambers and retractable awning, every aspect of the Colosseum was carefully designed to create the ultimate entertainment experience for the people of Rome. Even today, nearly two thousand years after it was built, the Colosseum remains an iconic symbol of the achievements of ancient Rome and a marvel of human engineering.

# Chapter 7: The Emperors Who Built the Colosseum

The story of the Colosseum cannot be told without understanding the crucial role played by the emperors who envisioned, commissioned, and oversaw its construction. The Colosseum, also known as the Flavian Amphitheater, was not just a colossal structure built to entertain the masses but a symbol of imperial power, ambition, and the ability to command the vast resources of the Roman Empire. Its construction spanned the reigns of three emperors: Vespasian, who initiated the project; his son Titus, who completed it; and Domitian, who added finishing touches and underground facilities. These emperors, all members of the Flavian dynasty, were responsible for transforming the Colosseum from a mere idea into a grand architectural wonder that continues to inspire awe thousands of years later.

The first emperor who played a central role in the creation of the Colosseum was Vespasian. Vespasian ascended to power in 69 AD after a period of political instability known as the Year of the Four Emperors, a year marked by civil wars, assassinations, and a succession of short-lived emperors. When Vespasian became emperor, he inherited a Rome that was in dire need of restoration and recovery. The previous emperor, Nero, had left a lasting scar on the city with his extravagant and self-serving rule, epitomized by his construction of the Domus Aurea, or "Golden House," a vast palace complex built on land that had been cleared by the Great Fire of Rome in 64 AD. This grand palace, complete with artificial lakes, sprawling gardens, and opulent rooms, was seen by the people of Rome as a symbol of Nero's selfishness and disregard for the public. While much of the city lay in ruins, Nero had focused on building a lavish palace for himself, further alienating the populace.

Vespasian, in contrast to Nero, sought to distance himself from this legacy of excess and to restore faith in the Roman leadership. One of his first major acts as emperor was to dismantle the Domus Aurea and repurpose the land it had occupied for public use. This decision was not only a practical one—returning land to the people—but also a powerful political statement. By building the Colosseum, a grand arena for public spectacles, on the site of Nero's private palace, Vespasian sought to demonstrate that his reign would be one of the people, for the people. The Colosseum was meant to stand as a monument to Roman power, unity, and generosity, a place where citizens from all walks of life could come together to witness the grandeur of the empire.

Vespasian initiated the construction of the Colosseum in 70 AD, a year after coming to power. The project was a massive undertaking that required enormous amounts of labor, materials, and logistical planning. It is believed that tens of thousands of slaves, many of them prisoners of war from Vespasian's military campaigns in Judea, were put to work building the colossal structure. The construction was financed, in part, by the spoils of war from the Jewish revolt, further tying the Colosseum to Vespasian's military successes. As a leader who prided himself on his military background, Vespasian understood the importance of using architecture to solidify his legacy and demonstrate the strength of the Roman Empire. The Colosseum, with its grand scale and innovative design, was intended to serve as a lasting symbol of Roman authority and the emperor's commitment to his people.

However, Vespasian would not live to see the completion of the Colosseum. He died in 79 AD, leaving the project in the hands of his eldest son, Titus. Titus, who had been a successful military commander, particularly during the Jewish rebellion, assumed the role of emperor after his father's death. Though his reign was short, lasting only two years, Titus is remembered for completing the Colosseum and opening it to the public in a grand ceremony that showcased the might and splendor of Rome. The dedication of the Colosseum took place in

80 AD and was marked by a series of elaborate games and spectacles that lasted for 100 days. These events included gladiatorial combats, wild animal hunts, and mock naval battles, all of which were staged to entertain the masses and celebrate the new emperor's achievement.

The opening games of the Colosseum under Titus were designed to awe and impress. The spectacle was unprecedented, with thousands of gladiators fighting to the death, wild animals brought from across the empire, and lavish displays of Roman military prowess. The games were not merely for entertainment but served a deeper political purpose. They reinforced the idea that the emperor was a benevolent ruler, providing the people with grand spectacles that showcased the empire's wealth and power. For Titus, these games were an opportunity to solidify his position as emperor and to gain the favor of the Roman populace. The completion of the Colosseum under his reign also allowed Titus to establish himself as a worthy successor to his father and to continue the Flavian legacy of public works and military triumphs.

Unfortunately, Titus' reign was marred by a series of disasters, including the eruption of Mount Vesuvius in 79 AD, which destroyed the cities of Pompeii and Herculaneum, and a devastating fire that swept through Rome in 80 AD. Despite these challenges, Titus remained popular with the people, in part due to his role in completing the Colosseum and his efforts to provide relief to those affected by these disasters. His untimely death in 81 AD meant that the Colosseum was still not entirely finished. While the main structure had been completed, additional features, such as the underground chambers and other facilities, still needed work.

It was under the reign of Domitian, Titus' younger brother, that the Colosseum was finally completed in its entirety. Domitian, who ruled from 81 to 96 AD, was the third and final emperor of the Flavian dynasty. While his reign is often remembered for its authoritarian nature and his eventual assassination, Domitian made significant contributions to the Colosseum. He expanded the structure by adding the hypogeum, the complex network of underground tunnels and chambers beneath the arena floor. These tunnels housed gladiators, animals, and stage machinery, allowing for dramatic entrances and surprises during the games. The hypogeum was a marvel of engineering, with elevators and pulleys that enabled animals and combatants to be raised directly into the arena, creating a more dynamic and thrilling experience for spectators.

In addition to the hypogeum, Domitian also added a third tier of seating to the Colosseum, increasing its capacity and allowing even more citizens to attend the games. This expansion was a reflection of Domitian's desire to be seen as a ruler who provided for the people, even as he tightened his grip on power and became increasingly paranoid and reclusive. The completion of the Colosseum under Domitian's rule ensured that the structure would stand as a lasting symbol of the Flavian dynasty's achievements, both in terms of architecture and public works.

The construction of the Colosseum by the Flavian emperors was not merely an architectural project but a carefully calculated political strategy. Each emperor used the Colosseum to shape his public image and to connect with the people of Rome in a way that previous emperors, particularly Nero, had failed to do. Vespasian's decision to build the Colosseum on the site of Nero's private palace was a powerful statement of his commitment to restoring Rome to its former glory and of his dedication to serving the people rather than indulging in personal luxury. Titus' completion of the Colosseum and the grand spectacles he organized for its opening cemented his reputation as a popular and generous ruler, despite the natural disasters that plagued his reign. Domitian's contributions, though made during a time of increasing political repression, ensured that the Colosseum would remain a functional and impressive structure for generations to come.

In conclusion, the Colosseum stands as a monument not only to the architectural and engineering prowess of ancient Rome but also to the political acumen of the Flavian emperors who built it. Each emperor contributed to the construction and completion of the Colosseum, leaving behind a legacy that would endure for centuries. The Colosseum became a symbol of imperial power, a place where the might of Rome was displayed for all to see, and a testament to the ability of the Flavian dynasty to command the resources and labor needed to build one of the most iconic structures in history. Through their vision, determination, and political savvy, Vespasian, Titus, and Domitian transformed the Colosseum from a dream into a reality, ensuring that their names would be forever associated with one of the greatest architectural achievements of the ancient world.

# Chapter 8: The Spectacular Naval Battles in the Arena

The Colosseum, one of the most iconic and recognizable structures of the ancient world, was known for its grand spectacles that entertained Roman citizens in ways that pushed the boundaries of engineering, imagination, and even the sheer audacity of human ingenuity. Among the most remarkable and awe-inspiring of these events were the mock naval battles, or *naumachiae*, held within the arena. The idea of recreating full-scale sea battles on land in the middle of a massive amphitheater, complete with ships, water, and combatants, sounds almost too incredible to believe. Yet, for a time, the Colosseum was the site of such spectacles, which served as a powerful testament to Rome's dominance over both land and sea.

The naval battles in the Colosseum were not merely for entertainment; they were deeply symbolic of Rome's mastery over nature and its imperial might. By staging these battles, the emperors sought to demonstrate their control over the elements, showing that even the vast forces of water could be tamed and manipulated for the amusement of the Roman people. The spectacle of watching ships sail into combat within the heart of Rome, far from the coasts or rivers where such vessels would naturally be found, was a reminder of Rome's far-reaching power and its ability to conquer not only foreign lands but the natural world itself.

The first recorded mock naval battle in Rome predates the construction of the Colosseum, with Julius Caesar famously staging a massive *naumachia* in 46 BC as part of his celebrations for his victories in Gaul and Egypt. He had a large artificial lake dug out in the Field of Mars, outside the city walls, and filled it with water for the battle. The combatants, often prisoners of war or condemned criminals, would reenact historical or legendary naval confrontations, fighting to the death as real Roman warships clashed on the artificial waters. These early *naumachiae* set the stage for later emperors, who would take the concept of naval spectacles to even grander heights.

When the Colosseum was constructed, the idea of staging naval battles in the amphitheater became a reality. The first known *naumachia* in the Colosseum took place during the reign of Emperor Titus, who inaugurated the amphitheater with a series of spectacular games and events in 80 AD. This included not only gladiatorial contests and wild animal hunts but also a mock naval battle that astonished the crowds. For this event, the arena floor was flooded with water, and specially designed ships were brought in to recreate a dramatic sea battle. These ships were often modeled after real Roman vessels, complete with sails, oars, and even soldiers who would engage in combat as the ships maneuvered within the limited space of the arena.

The logistics of flooding the Colosseum for such an event were nothing short of remarkable. The engineering required to transform the solid arena floor into a massive water basin capable of holding ships was a feat that showcased the brilliance of Roman architects and engineers. The Colosseum had an elaborate system of channels, pipes, and drains that allowed water to be brought in from nearby sources, such as aqueducts or reservoirs, and then removed once the battle was over. These systems were designed to fill the arena with water in a relatively short amount of time, transforming it from a sandy battlefield into a miniature sea. The sheer complexity of this operation demonstrated the Romans' advanced knowledge of hydraulics and their ability to manipulate water on a grand scale.

Once the arena was flooded, the naval battle would commence. The combatants, who were often prisoners or slaves condemned to die, would be divided into two opposing teams, each manning their respective ships. These ships were not just props but functional vessels, complete with rowers, sailors, and soldiers who would fight to the death on the water. The battles themselves were highly choreographed, often based on historical or mythical events, and were intended to entertain the crowd with their drama and spectacle. The ships would ram into each other, archers would fire arrows from the decks, and soldiers would board enemy vessels to engage in hand-to-hand combat. The battles were fierce and bloody, with the water often turning red from the wounds of the combatants.

Despite the violent nature of these battles, the Romans viewed them as an exhilarating form of entertainment, a way to experience the thrill of war without the actual risk. For the spectators, watching these naval battles unfold was an opportunity to witness the might of Rome's naval forces in action, even if the combatants were not professional soldiers. The sheer spectacle of seeing ships clashing in the middle of an amphitheater, surrounded by thousands of cheering spectators, must have been an unforgettable experience for those in attendance.

While Titus's inaugural *naumachia* in the Colosseum was the most famous, it was not the last. His successor, Domitian, also staged naval battles in the amphitheater, further refining the process of flooding and draining the arena. However, as time went on, the logistics and cost of staging such events became increasingly difficult to manage. The complexity of flooding the arena, maintaining the ships, and providing a steady supply of combatants made the naval battles less frequent. Eventually, the Colosseum's subterranean chambers, known as the hypogeum, were constructed under Domitian's reign. These underground tunnels and rooms housed gladiators, animals, and equipment for the more traditional spectacles, but they also made it difficult to flood the arena for naval battles. With the hypogeum in place, the practice of holding *naumachiae* in the Colosseum was largely abandoned, though the memory of these spectacular events lived on.

Despite their relative rarity, the naval battles in the Colosseum left an indelible mark on Roman culture and the legacy of the Flavian emperors who organized them. The *naumachiae* were a powerful display of imperial wealth and engineering prowess, serving as a reminder of Rome's dominance over both land and sea. The very act of transforming an amphitheater into a body of water, and then staging full-scale naval combat within it, was a statement of Rome's unparalleled ability to command the natural world and turn even the most extraordinary of ideas into reality. It also underscored the emperor's role as the ultimate provider of entertainment and spectacle for the people, using these events to win favor and solidify their authority.

In conclusion, the naval battles staged in the Colosseum were a unique and awe-inspiring form of entertainment that demonstrated the ingenuity and ambition of the Roman Empire. These battles, while rare, were a testament to the Romans' mastery of engineering, hydraulics, and spectacle. By flooding the Colosseum and recreating naval combat on such a grand scale, the emperors who organized these events cemented their legacies as rulers capable of providing extraordinary entertainment for their people. The *naumachiae* were more than just mock battles; they were a celebration of Roman power, a display of the empire's ability to conquer both land and sea, and a reminder of the grandeur that defined ancient Rome.

# Chapter 9: The Colosseum Through the Ages

The Colosseum, also known as the Flavian Amphitheater, has stood for nearly two millennia as one of the most iconic and enduring symbols of ancient Rome. Its imposing size, architectural grandeur, and association with the gladiatorial spectacles of the Roman Empire make it a testament to Roman engineering and a marvel of ancient construction. However, the Colosseum's history did not end with the fall of the Roman Empire. Over the centuries, it has experienced numerous transformations, surviving natural disasters, human neglect, and even repurposing for a variety of uses. Its journey through time is one of resilience and adaptability, mirroring the rise and fall of civilizations and the ebb and flow of cultural values. The Colosseum's story is one of survival against the odds, and its changing roles reflect the ways in which societies have interpreted and valued their heritage.

When the Colosseum was completed in 80 AD under Emperor Titus, it quickly became the heart of Roman public life. It was a place where emperors demonstrated their power, wealth, and benevolence by hosting games that could last for days or even months. Gladiators fought, wild animals were hunted, and sometimes mythological and historical events were reenacted in elaborate spectacles. The Colosseum could hold between 50,000 and 80,000 spectators, a staggering number for the time, and its advanced design allowed for the efficient movement of large crowds, with spectators being able to exit the structure within minutes. For over 400 years, the Colosseum served its original purpose, hosting events that catered to the entertainment desires of the Roman populace and reinforcing the power of the emperors who controlled it.

However, as the Roman Empire began to decline in the 5th century AD, so too did the use of the Colosseum. The fall of Rome in 476 AD marked the beginning of a period of upheaval in the Western Roman Empire, and with it, the grand spectacles that had once defined Roman culture became increasingly rare. The Western Empire collapsed, and with it, the economic and social structures that had supported the games. The Colosseum, which had once echoed with the roars of the crowd, gradually fell into disuse. The once-vibrant arena where gladiators fought for their lives became a ghost of its former self. By the 6th century, the Colosseum was no longer used for gladiatorial games, and the structure began to suffer from neglect and a lack of maintenance.

During this period of decline, the Colosseum faced not only human neglect but also natural disasters. Rome experienced several devastating earthquakes in the following centuries, which weakened and damaged the structure. One of the most significant earthquakes occurred in 1349, which caused much of the southern side of the Colosseum to collapse. The massive stones that had once formed the outer walls were hauled away and repurposed for other building projects throughout Rome. This practice of using the Colosseum as a quarry was not uncommon in the Middle Ages. The fallen stones were used to construct buildings such as churches, palaces, and other public structures, contributing to the fragmentation and deterioration of the once-majestic amphitheater.

In addition to its use as a source of building materials, the Colosseum was repurposed for various other functions during the medieval period. One of the most intriguing chapters in its history was its transformation into a fortress. As the power of the Roman Empire faded and Rome became a patchwork of competing factions, noble families sought to fortify their holdings against rival groups. The Colosseum, with its sturdy walls and strategic location, became a desirable stronghold. By the 12th century, the powerful Frangipani family had taken control of the Colosseum, using it as a fortress to defend their interests in the city. The amphitheater, once a symbol of public entertainment and imperial grandeur, now served as a stronghold for feudal warfare, a far cry from its original purpose.

Another surprising development in the Colosseum's history came when it was partially converted into a Christian site. As Christianity spread throughout the Roman Empire in the centuries following its fall, attitudes toward the Colosseum began to change. The games that had once taken place in the amphitheater, particularly the gladiatorial contests and executions, were viewed as barbaric and incompatible with Christian values. Over time, the Colosseum became associated with the early Christian martyrs who, according to some historical accounts, were executed within its walls during periods of persecution. Although there is limited historical evidence to support the claim that Christians were martyred in the Colosseum itself, the legend grew, and by the Middle Ages, the amphitheater was seen as a sacred site. Pope Benedict XIV consecrated the Colosseum in the 18th century, dedicating it to the memory of the Christian martyrs who were believed to have died there. Crosses were erected within the structure, and religious processions were held, transforming the Colosseum from a place of bloodshed to one of reverence.

Throughout the Renaissance and into the early modern period, the Colosseum continued to attract attention, though its condition remained precarious. Artists, scholars, and travelers from across Europe marveled at the ruins of ancient Rome, and the Colosseum became a symbol of the lost grandeur of the classical world. The Renaissance was a period of rediscovery of ancient art and architecture, and the Colosseum, along with other Roman ruins, played a key role in inspiring a revival of classical ideals. The amphitheater was sketched by artists such as Michelangelo, and its massive, crumbling arches were seen as a reminder of the fragility of human achievements and the passage of time.

Despite its symbolic importance, the Colosseum remained in a state of disrepair for much of this period. Successive popes and Roman leaders showed varying degrees of interest in preserving it, but it was not until the 19th century that serious efforts were made to protect and restore the structure. The rise of Romanticism in the 18th and 19th centuries, with its emphasis on the sublime beauty of ruins and the grandeur of the past, further cemented the Colosseum's status as a cultural icon. By this time, the amphitheater had become a popular destination for European travelers on the Grand Tour, a tradition of cultural and educational travel that exposed the elites of Europe to the classical world.

In the 19th century, under the influence of Romanticism and a growing sense of historical preservation, efforts to stabilize and restore the Colosseum began in earnest. Italian authorities, along with various cultural organizations, recognized the importance of the Colosseum not only as a monument of Rome's imperial past but also as a symbol of Italy's cultural heritage. As Italy moved toward unification in the 19th century, the Colosseum came to represent not just the power of ancient Rome but also the potential for a unified Italy. National pride in the country's Roman past led to increased efforts to preserve the structure, and restorations were undertaken to prevent further deterioration.

The 20th century brought with it new challenges and opportunities for the Colosseum. During World War II, Rome was heavily bombed, and while the Colosseum was not directly targeted, the city around it suffered significant damage. The amphitheater stood as a silent witness to the violence and destruction of the war, much as it had witnessed the upheavals of previous centuries. After the war, further restorations were undertaken, and the Colosseum became a symbol of peace and endurance. In 1980, it was designated a UNESCO World Heritage Site, ensuring that it would receive international recognition and protection for generations to come.

Today, the Colosseum continues to draw millions of visitors each year, serving as one of the most popular tourist destinations in the world. While it no longer serves as a venue for gladiatorial combat or public spectacles, it remains a place where people come to reflect on the grandeur of ancient Rome and the long history of the structure itself. Ongoing preservation efforts have helped to stabilize the Colosseum and protect it from further damage, though challenges remain. Pollution, the wear and tear of millions of visitors, and the passage of time all pose threats to the structure, but the commitment to preserving this symbol of Rome's past remains strong.

In recent years, the Colosseum has taken on new roles as well. It has been used for cultural events, performances, and even political statements. In particular, the amphitheater has become a symbol of the fight against capital punishment. Each year, the Colosseum is lit up to mark the global campaign against the death penalty, a poignant reminder of the many lives that were lost within its walls during the days of gladiatorial combat and public executions. This modern use of the Colosseum as a symbol of peace and justice stands in stark contrast to its ancient role as a venue for violent spectacles, demonstrating how the meanings of historical monuments can change over time.

The Colosseum's journey through the ages is a story of resilience, adaptation, and transformation. From its early days as a symbol of imperial power and public entertainment, to its use as a fortress, a religious site, and a symbol of national identity, the Colosseum has survived the rise and fall of empires, the ravages of time, and the changing values of societies. Today, it stands not only as a testament to the architectural and engineering achievements of ancient Rome but also as a symbol of the enduring power of history to shape and inspire the present. Its continued preservation and relevance remind us of the importance of protecting our cultural heritage, even as we reinterpret it for future generations.

# Chapter 10: The Role of the Colosseum in Roman Society

The Colosseum, or the Flavian Amphitheater as it was originally known, played a profound and multifaceted role in Roman society, making it one of the most significant public spaces in ancient Rome. Its construction began under Emperor Vespasian around 70-72 AD and was completed in 80 AD by his son and successor, Emperor Titus. It quickly became a central feature of Roman life, symbolizing the power and grandeur of the Roman Empire while also serving as a stage for events that deeply reflected the values, culture, and politics of Roman society.

One of the primary functions of the Colosseum was to provide entertainment to the masses. In an era before the invention of modern forms of media, the amphitheater served as the ultimate venue for public spectacles. The games hosted at the Colosseum, including gladiatorial combat, wild animal hunts, and executions, were designed to entertain and distract the Roman populace. These spectacles, known as "ludi," were often free to attend, a fact that endeared the emperors to the people and helped ensure the loyalty of the masses. By sponsoring these games, emperors demonstrated their generosity, solidified their political power, and reinforced social cohesion in a vast and diverse empire.

The games themselves were far more than mere entertainment. They were a potent tool for social control, offering the Roman government a way to pacify and placate the population. The concept of "bread and circuses," or "panem et circenses," coined by the poet Juvenal, encapsulates this strategy. Roman rulers understood that keeping the people fed and entertained was crucial to maintaining order and preventing unrest. By providing these distractions, the government could deflect attention away from more pressing issues, such as poverty, inequality, and political corruption. The Colosseum, therefore, was a critical venue for maintaining the stability of Roman society by diverting public focus from the hardships of daily life.

The events held at the Colosseum were also an expression of Roman values, particularly the ideals of strength, bravery, and martial prowess. Gladiatorial combat, the most famous of the spectacles, embodied the virtues that Roman society revered. Gladiators were celebrated for their courage and skill in combat, and the arena became a place where individuals could achieve fame and honor, even if they were often slaves or prisoners of war. The brutality of these combats, in which men fought to the death, reflected the harsh realities of Roman life and the glorification of military conquest and dominance. The Colosseum was, in many ways, a microcosm of the Roman Empire itself—a place where the strong triumphed over the weak, and where violence was not only accepted but celebrated as a means of asserting power.

In addition to showcasing individual valor, the Colosseum's spectacles also reinforced the collective strength of the Roman state. Many of the events were designed to demonstrate Rome's military might and its ability to conquer and subdue foreign peoples and lands. Wild animal hunts, or "venationes," were a common feature of the games, in which exotic animals from the farthest reaches of the empire were brought to the Colosseum to be hunted or executed by trained fighters. These animals, such as lions, elephants, tigers, and rhinoceroses, symbolized the vastness of the Roman Empire and its dominion over nature and foreign territories. The presence of these creatures in the arena was a powerful reminder to Roman citizens of their empire's greatness and its ability to control even the most ferocious of beasts. The spectacle of taming or killing these animals mirrored the subjugation of Rome's enemies, reinforcing the idea of Roman superiority and imperial power.

The Colosseum was also a political tool for emperors seeking to bolster their popularity and legitimacy. By hosting lavish games, emperors could present themselves as benefactors of the people, ensuring their favor and loyalty. For many emperors, especially those whose claim to power was tenuous, the Colosseum provided an opportunity to display their wealth, generosity, and commitment to Roman traditions. The inaugural games held by Emperor Titus in 80 AD, for instance, were a grand affair lasting 100 days and included a wide array of spectacles, from gladiatorial combat to wild animal hunts and even mock naval battles. These games were a crucial way for Titus to establish his rule after the death of his father Vespasian and to signal the stability and strength of his reign.

The games also offered emperors a means of communicating political messages. Many of the events in the Colosseum were highly symbolic, reflecting the emperor's control over life and death. Executions of criminals and prisoners of war were a common spectacle, and the way in which these executions were staged often had a deeper meaning. For instance, criminals might be executed in ways that reenacted famous myths or historical events, with the victims playing the roles of condemned figures from Rome's past. This not only provided entertainment but also served as a warning to anyone who might challenge the authority of the emperor. The Colosseum, in this sense, was not just a place of entertainment but also a stage for political theater, where the power of the emperor was displayed in full view of the public.

The hierarchical structure of Roman society was also reflected in the seating arrangements within the Colosseum. The amphitheater was carefully designed to reinforce the social order, with seating divided according to rank and status. The emperor, senators, and other elite members of society were given the best seats, closest to the action, while the lower classes were seated further back. Women, except for the Vestal Virgins, were relegated to the upper tiers, a clear reflection of their subordinate position in Roman society. The seating arrangements at the Colosseum mirrored the broader social hierarchy of the empire, reminding spectators of their place within the rigid structure of Roman life.

While the Colosseum served as a venue for mass entertainment, it also had religious and ceremonial functions. Many of the games were dedicated to the gods, and the amphitheater was sometimes used for ceremonies that honored Roman deities or celebrated military victories. The emperor himself was often viewed as a divine figure, and his presence at the games further reinforced the link between the imperial office and the gods. In this way, the Colosseum became a space where the divine and the mortal intersected, and where the emperor's role as both ruler and religious figure was reaffirmed.

The role of the Colosseum in Roman society extended beyond its immediate use as a venue for entertainment and political spectacle. It was also an architectural marvel that reflected the engineering prowess and artistic ambition of the Roman Empire. The sheer size of the structure, combined with its complex system of vaults, arches, and corridors, made it a symbol of Roman ingenuity and mastery over the physical world. The Colosseum's design allowed it to hold tens of thousands of spectators, and its ability to manage large crowds efficiently was a testament to Roman organizational skill. The amphitheater's construction, using materials such as concrete, travertine, and tufa, demonstrated Rome's ability to create monumental structures that could stand the test of time. The Colosseum was not just a place for games; it was a symbol of Roman civilization itself, a manifestation of the empire's values, power, and technological achievement.

Over time, the Colosseum's role in Roman society evolved as the empire itself changed. By the late 4th and early 5th centuries, as Christianity became the dominant religion in the Roman Empire, the gladiatorial games and other violent spectacles began to lose favor.

Christian leaders viewed these events as barbaric and incompatible with their teachings, and over time, the Colosseum's role as a venue for bloodshed diminished. The rise of Christianity marked a significant shift in Roman values, and the Colosseum, once the heart of Roman public life, gradually fell into disuse.

Nevertheless, the Colosseum remained an enduring symbol of Rome's imperial past. Even as it was repurposed in later centuries—used as a quarry for building materials, a fortress for noble families, and eventually a religious site dedicated to Christian martyrs—it retained its connection to the grandeur and power of ancient Rome. Today, the Colosseum stands not only as a reminder of the role it played in Roman society but also as a monument to the complexities of that society—the interplay of power, violence, entertainment, religion, and social order that defined the Roman Empire at its height.

The Colosseum's role in Roman society was multifaceted and deeply embedded in the political, social, and cultural fabric of the empire. It served as a tool of social control, a means of reinforcing Roman values, and a stage for political theater. Its architectural brilliance symbolized the technological and artistic achievements of Rome, while its spectacles reflected the empire's military might and the emperor's power over life and death. As both an entertainment venue and a political institution, the Colosseum played a central role in shaping the identity of Roman society, leaving a lasting legacy that continues to captivate the world today.

# Chapter 11: How the Colosseum Was Constructed

The construction of the Colosseum, or the Flavian Amphitheater as it was initially called, stands as one of the most monumental engineering achievements of ancient Rome. Erected between 70 and 80 AD under the reigns of the emperors Vespasian and Titus, this colossal structure symbolizes the grandeur and might of the Roman Empire. The process of building such a massive amphitheater, which could hold tens of thousands of spectators, required not only advanced engineering and architectural skills but also enormous resources in terms of labor, materials, and logistics. The Colosseum's construction was a demonstration of Rome's ability to marshal its wealth, technology, and manpower to create structures that would both serve the public and immortalize the power of the empire.

The Colosseum was commissioned by Emperor Vespasian shortly after he came to power in 69 AD, during a period of turmoil known as the Year of the Four Emperors. His decision to build the amphitheater in the heart of Rome was a calculated political move. The construction of such a grand public structure served multiple purposes: it demonstrated the new emperor's commitment to the people, reinforced the stability of his reign after a period of civil war, and reasserted the dominance of the Flavian dynasty. By choosing to build the Colosseum on the site of Nero's former palace, the Domus Aurea, Vespasian also made a symbolic gesture of giving the land back to the Roman people, transforming what had been an imperial pleasure ground into a space for public entertainment.

The location of the Colosseum was not only significant for its political symbolism but also for its practicality. Situated on the site of a drained artificial lake that had once been part of Nero's sprawling palace complex, the land provided a large, flat area ideal for the construction of such a massive structure. Additionally, the location was central, making it accessible to the Roman populace and near other important landmarks such as the Roman Forum. The decision to drain the lake was no small feat and required advanced knowledge of hydrology and engineering. The Romans redirected water channels and built drainage systems to ensure the area remained dry, thus laying the groundwork for the amphitheater.

The foundation of the Colosseum was a critical aspect of its construction, given the sheer size and weight of the structure. The Romans dug a deep circular trench, about 12 meters wide, which was then filled with concrete to create a stable base. Concrete, a material the Romans had perfected, played a central role in the construction of the Colosseum. Roman concrete, known as "opus caementicium," was made from a mixture of lime, volcanic ash, and small stones. Its strength, durability, and ability to harden underwater made it ideal for large-scale building projects like the Colosseum. The use of concrete allowed the Romans to create the immense foundations and vaulted structures that supported the amphitheater's massive weight, ensuring its stability for centuries to come.

Once the foundations were laid, the construction of the Colosseum's superstructure began. The Colosseum is an elliptical structure, measuring approximately 189 meters long and 156 meters wide, with a height of around 48 meters. It was designed as a freestanding building, in contrast to earlier Greek amphitheaters, which were often built into hillsides for structural support. This presented a unique engineering challenge, as the entire weight of the structure had to be supported by the walls and the internal framework. The outer walls of the Colosseum were built using massive blocks of travertine, a type of limestone quarried from Tivoli, about 20 miles outside of Rome. These blocks, some weighing several tons, were transported to the construction site via a network of roads and rivers, a logistical feat that required careful planning and organization.

The travertine blocks were held together not by mortar but by iron clamps, which provided additional strength and flexibility. This technique was crucial for a structure as large as the Colosseum, as it allowed for slight shifts in the masonry without causing significant damage. The use of iron clamps also sped up the construction process, as it eliminated the need for long drying times associated with mortar. The exterior of the Colosseum was adorned with three levels of arches, each decorated with half-columns in the Tuscan, Ionic, and Corinthian orders, which added both strength and beauty to the structure. These arches not only supported the weight of the upper tiers but also created open spaces that allowed for better crowd flow in and out of the amphitheater.

The Colosseum's internal structure was equally remarkable. The seating area, or "cavea," was designed to accommodate over 50,000 spectators, with seating arranged in a tiered system according to social class. The lower seats, closest to the arena, were reserved for senators and other elite members of Roman society, while the upper tiers were for the lower classes and women. The seating was built on a complex system of concrete vaults and arches, which distributed the weight of the structure evenly and allowed for easy movement of spectators throughout the building. The vomitoria, or entrances and exits, were strategically placed to allow large crowds to enter and exit the amphitheater quickly, a feature that has influenced the design of modern stadiums.

The arena itself was a marvel of Roman engineering. It was an elliptical space covered with sand, which helped absorb the blood from the violent spectacles that took place there. Beneath the arena lay a complex network of underground chambers and passageways, known as the hypogeum, which housed gladiators, animals, and stage machinery. The hypogeum was equipped with trapdoors and elevators that allowed for dramatic entrances and exits during the games. The construction of this underground system required advanced knowledge of mechanics and hydraulics, as the Romans devised ways to raise and lower cages and platforms from the hypogeum to the arena floor.

The Colosseum also featured an elaborate system of awnings, or the "velarium," which protected spectators from the sun and rain. The velarium was a retractable canvas canopy that was operated by a team of sailors from the Roman navy, who were stationed on top of the Colosseum. The canopy was anchored to a series of masts placed around the perimeter of the amphitheater, and ropes were used to raise and lower the fabric. This system not only provided shade but also demonstrated the ingenuity of Roman engineering in solving the challenges of such a large, open-air structure.

The construction of the Colosseum required a massive workforce, including skilled laborers, engineers, architects, and unskilled slaves. Many of the laborers were slaves captured during the Jewish Wars, particularly after the siege of Jerusalem in 70 AD, which provided both the labor and much of the wealth needed to finance the project. The construction of the Colosseum was a monumental undertaking, and it is estimated that thousands of workers toiled for nearly a decade to complete the amphitheater. The scale of the project, the precision of the engineering, and the sheer amount of resources required were a testament to the organizational abilities of the Roman state and its capacity to mobilize human and material resources on an unprecedented scale.

By 80 AD, under Emperor Titus, the Colosseum was completed and inaugurated with a series of lavish games that lasted for 100 days. These games included gladiatorial combat, wild animal hunts, and even mock naval battles, which showcased the versatility of the amphitheater's design. The inauguration of the Colosseum was not only a celebration of the building itself but also a demonstration of the might and splendor of the Roman Empire. The Colosseum quickly became the center of public life in Rome, hosting games and spectacles that drew thousands of spectators from across the empire.

In the centuries that followed, the Colosseum continued to serve as a venue for public entertainment, although its role evolved over time. By the late Roman Empire, gladiatorial games had fallen out of favor, and the Colosseum was used more for animal hunts and executions. In the Middle Ages, the structure fell into disrepair and was repurposed for various uses, including as a fortress, a quarry for building materials, and a Christian shrine. Despite this, the Colosseum remained an enduring symbol of Rome's architectural and engineering prowess.

The construction of the Colosseum was a monumental achievement that reflected the values and ambitions of the Roman Empire. It was a building designed not only to entertain but also to showcase the power, wealth, and technological mastery of ancient Rome. The Colosseum's grandeur and scale were unparalleled at the time, and its construction required innovative engineering solutions, meticulous planning, and an enormous investment of resources.

The amphitheater stood as a symbol of the Flavian dynasty's commitment to the Roman people, offering them a grand space where they could witness spectacular events that celebrated Roman military conquests, valor, and even the divine status of the emperor. The political motivations behind the construction were evident, as it was a way to stabilize and solidify the rule of Vespasian and his successors by currying favor with the masses through public entertainment.

The selection of materials played a critical role in ensuring the Colosseum's longevity. In addition to travertine, the Romans used tufa, a soft volcanic rock, for the substructure and some interior walls, as well as brick and concrete for vaults and arches. The clever combination of materials contributed to the strength and durability of the structure, which has allowed the Colosseum to survive earthquakes, fires, and centuries of wear and tear. The innovative use of arches and vaults, fundamental elements of Roman architecture, distributed the weight of the structure efficiently and allowed for its immense size.

The logistics behind transporting the building materials to the Colosseum's construction site were another significant feat. The travertine blocks used for the outer wall, weighing several tons each, were transported from the quarries in Tivoli using a combination of ox-drawn carts and rafts along the Tiber River. Once at the site, the blocks were precisely cut and fitted without the use of mortar, relying on iron clamps to hold them in place. This technique allowed the structure to remain flexible, which was crucial in preventing collapse during minor earthquakes.

Furthermore, the Romans employed an impressive workforce for the construction. Skilled artisans and architects were responsible for designing and supervising the construction, while the labor-intensive tasks were performed by thousands of enslaved people, many of whom were prisoners of war. These slaves not only provided the manual labor required for excavation, stone-cutting, and hauling materials but also participated in the construction of the intricate systems that supported the Colosseum's various functions.

One of the most remarkable aspects of the Colosseum's construction was the underground complex known as the hypogeum. This subterranean network of tunnels and chambers housed gladiators, animals, and stage machinery used during the games. Engineers designed a sophisticated system of elevators and pulleys, operated by human power, to raise animals and fighters from the hypogeum to the arena floor. This allowed for dramatic reveals and surprise elements during the games, adding to the excitement and unpredictability of the spectacles. The hypogeum was a marvel of Roman engineering, illustrating the empire's advanced understanding of mechanics and hydraulics.

In addition to the hypogeum, the Romans devised a retractable roof system, the "velarium," which provided shade for spectators. The velarium consisted of a large canvas awning that could be extended over the seating areas to protect against the sun and rain. The awning was supported by a series of poles and ropes anchored to the top of the Colosseum's outer wall. Sailors from the Roman navy were responsible for operating the velarium, using their expertise in rigging and knot-tying to manipulate the massive structure. This ingenious system allowed spectators to enjoy the games in relative comfort, regardless of the weather conditions.

The tiered seating arrangement of the Colosseum also reflected Roman society's rigid social hierarchy. The most prestigious seats were located closest to the arena, reserved for senators, high-ranking officials, and the emperor himself. Behind them sat the equestrians, or the Roman knights, followed by the general populace, with the poorest citizens, women, and slaves seated in the uppermost sections. This division of seating ensured that social distinctions were maintained, even in a public venue, and reinforced the stratified nature of Roman society.

The construction of the Colosseum was completed in a remarkably short period of time for such a massive structure. The project, which began under Vespasian, was largely completed by 80 AD, during the reign of his son Titus. Titus marked the completion of the amphitheater with an extravagant inaugural festival that lasted 100 days, during which gladiatorial games, animal hunts, and mock naval battles were held. These events demonstrated the versatility of the Colosseum's design and its ability to accommodate a wide range of spectacles, from intimate combat to large-scale reenactments of naval battles.

The Colosseum's influence extended far beyond the borders of Rome. It served as a model for amphitheaters and stadiums throughout the Roman Empire, many of which were built in provincial cities to provide similar forms of entertainment for the local population. The Roman Empire was vast, and by replicating the Colosseum's design, the Romans exported their cultural and architectural ideals to distant regions, reinforcing the power and influence of the empire.

Over time, however, the role of the Colosseum in Roman life evolved. By the late Roman Empire, as Christianity became the dominant religion, gladiatorial games and other violent spectacles fell out of favor. The rise of Christian morality and the church's condemnation of the bloodshed and cruelty associated with the games led to the eventual decline of the Colosseum's use as an arena for public entertainment. By the 5th century, the gladiatorial games had largely ceased, although animal hunts and executions continued sporadically. In the centuries that followed, the Colosseum suffered from neglect, looting, and natural disasters, including several earthquakes that caused significant damage to the structure.

Despite its decline, the Colosseum remained a potent symbol of Rome's imperial past. During the Middle Ages, parts of the amphitheater were repurposed for various uses, including as a fortress for noble families and as a quarry for stone and other building materials. The Colosseum's stones were used to construct several buildings in Rome, including churches and palaces, further embedding the amphitheater into the fabric of the city.

In the Renaissance and Baroque periods, the Colosseum became a subject of fascination for architects, artists, and scholars. Its ruined state was romanticized as a testament to the grandeur of ancient Rome, and it inspired many to study and revive classical architectural styles. By the 18th century, the Colosseum was being recognized as a historical monument, and efforts were made to preserve and restore it. Today, the Colosseum stands not only as a relic of ancient Rome but also as a UNESCO World Heritage Site and one of the most visited tourist attractions in the world.

In conclusion, the construction of the Colosseum was a remarkable achievement that showcased the engineering prowess, political ambition, and cultural values of the Roman Empire. Its design, materials, and scale were a testament to Rome's technological and logistical capabilities, while its role as a public entertainment venue reinforced the social and political order of the empire. Though it has undergone significant changes over the centuries, the Colosseum remains an enduring symbol of Rome's greatness, a monument to the empire's architectural ingenuity and its complex relationship with power, violence, and public spectacle.

# Chapter 12: The Colosseum's Place in Roman Architecture

The Colosseum holds an unrivaled place in the architectural heritage of ancient Rome, representing not only a monumental achievement in engineering and construction but also a reflection of the socio-political values that defined Roman culture. As one of the most iconic structures from the Roman Empire, the Colosseum, or Flavian Amphitheater, exemplifies the grand scale, ingenuity, and practicality that characterized Roman architecture. It is a masterpiece that blends form and function, constructed to both awe its viewers and serve a specific purpose: to host public spectacles that entertained and reinforced the power of the Roman state. The architectural significance of the Colosseum can be understood by examining its design, construction techniques, engineering advancements, and its enduring influence on both ancient and modern architecture.

At its core, the Colosseum's design was a response to the needs of a vast, growing population in the city of Rome. By the time the amphitheater was commissioned by Emperor Vespasian around 70 AD, Rome had become the thriving heart of an empire that spanned three continents. The city itself was teeming with citizens, freedmen, slaves, and foreigners, all of whom needed public spaces where they could gather, socialize, and engage in the collective cultural experience that defined Roman life. The Colosseum was built not only to accommodate vast numbers of spectators but to give them an immersive experience in a setting that emphasized Rome's organizational and technological prowess. The design of the Colosseum, therefore, aimed to maximize the number of spectators it could hold—estimated at over 50,000—while ensuring ease of access, efficient crowd control, and unobstructed views for all attendees.

One of the most defining features of the Colosseum's architecture is its elliptical shape, which was a departure from earlier theaters and amphitheaters that were often circular or semi-circular in design. The elliptical form allowed for a more dynamic and engaging viewing experience by ensuring that spectators, regardless of their position in the stands, had a clear line of sight to the center of the arena. This practical aspect of the design also symbolized the inclusivity of Roman entertainment, which was intended to unite people of different classes and backgrounds in a shared experience of spectacle. The Colosseum was a place where the emperor and the common citizen could sit (albeit in vastly different sections) and enjoy the same events, an architectural reflection of the Roman ideal of "bread and circuses" — keeping the populace content through public games and entertainment.

The exterior design of the Colosseum was just as striking as its interior layout. The facade, built primarily of travertine stone, was an imposing four-story structure that stood nearly 50 meters tall. Each of the first three stories featured 80 arched entrances, supported by a series of half-columns in the Tuscan, Ionic, and Corinthian orders, a design that symbolized the progression from simplicity to refinement in Roman architectural principles. This use of the three classical orders of columns on the exterior was a common feature in Roman public architecture and reflected the Romans' admiration for Greek architecture while adding their own practical modifications. The arches not only provided structural support but also contributed to the aesthetic grandeur of the building, creating a sense of rhythm and harmony that echoed the ideals of Roman order and control.

The use of the arch was a cornerstone of Roman architectural innovation, and the Colosseum represents one of the finest examples of how this feature was used to create large, open spaces while distributing weight evenly throughout the structure. The combination of arches and vaults—another key Roman invention—allowed the Colosseum to be built as a freestanding structure, in contrast to earlier Greek theaters, which were typically built into hillsides for support. The Colosseum's complex network of arches and vaults not only made the building more stable but also allowed for the efficient flow of people in and out of the amphitheater. The "vomitoria," or passageways, were strategically placed to enable large crowds to enter and exit the Colosseum quickly, reducing the risk of congestion or stampedes. This practical innovation in crowd control has influenced the design of modern stadiums and public arenas.

The Colosseum also demonstrated the Romans' mastery of concrete, an innovative material that allowed for the construction of large-scale structures like never before. Roman concrete, made from a mixture of lime mortar, volcanic sand, and small stones, was both strong and flexible, making it ideal for supporting the massive weight of the Colosseum. This material allowed the architects to construct the Colosseum's intricate system of vaults and arches with greater speed and efficiency than traditional stone construction methods. The interior of the Colosseum, much of which was built using concrete, featured an extensive network of corridors, stairways, and seating areas, all designed to provide spectators with easy access to their seats while ensuring the structural integrity of the building.

The seating arrangement inside the Colosseum was another architectural marvel that reflected the strict hierarchy of Roman society. The "cavea," or seating area, was divided into three main sections: the podium, the maenianum primum, and the maenianum secundum. The podium, located closest to the arena, was reserved for senators, magistrates, and other elite members of Roman society. The maenianum primum, the next tier of seating, was designated for the equestrian class, while the maenianum secundum, the uppermost tier, was reserved for the general populace, including women and slaves. This tiered seating arrangement not only reinforced social distinctions but also ensured that each group had a designated space within the amphitheater, reflecting the highly structured nature of Roman life.

The architecture of the Colosseum was, in this sense, a physical manifestation of Rome's rigid class system.

The Colosseum's underground chambers, known as the hypogeum, added another layer of complexity to its architectural design. This network of tunnels, passageways, and holding cells beneath the arena floor housed gladiators, wild animals, and stage machinery used during the games. The hypogeum was an ingenious feature that allowed for dramatic entrances and exits, with trapdoors and lifts enabling animals and performers to suddenly appear in the middle of the arena. The Romans even developed an elaborate system of pulleys and levers to move props, scenery, and combatants, creating a spectacle that was as much a feat of engineering as it was entertainment. The hypogeum's design illustrates the Romans' ability to integrate mechanical and architectural innovations into their buildings, enhancing the overall experience for spectators.

The Colosseum's engineering feats extended beyond the arena itself. The Romans were also able to create an intricate system of drains and sewers to manage the flow of water in and around the amphitheater. This was especially important given the Colosseum's location on the site of an artificial lake that had once been part of Nero's palace complex. The Romans constructed a sophisticated drainage system to prevent flooding and ensure that the arena floor remained dry, even during heavy rain. This hydraulic engineering was a testament to the Romans' advanced understanding of water management, which was crucial in a city as large and densely populated as Rome.

As part of the broader architectural landscape of Rome, the Colosseum was both a product of its time and a model for future public buildings. It reflected the values of the Flavian dynasty, who used monumental architecture to legitimize their rule and win the favor of the people. The construction of the Colosseum signaled a shift in Roman architecture towards grand public spaces that were designed to impress, entertain, and unite the populace. It also demonstrated the Roman state's ability to mobilize vast resources, including labor, materials, and technology, to construct buildings that would stand as symbols of the empire's power and endurance.

In the centuries that followed its construction, the Colosseum influenced the design of amphitheaters and public spaces throughout the Roman Empire. Cities across the provinces, from Gaul to North Africa, constructed their own versions of the Colosseum, adapting its design to local contexts but preserving the essential elements that made it a functional and symbolic space. The amphitheater became a defining feature of Roman urban planning, serving as a center for civic life and a stage for public displays of power, whether through gladiatorial games, executions, or animal hunts. The legacy of the Colosseum's architectural design continued to shape Roman public buildings long after the decline of the empire.

In modern times, the Colosseum remains a source of inspiration for architects and engineers. Its combination of structural innovation, aesthetic beauty, and practical functionality has influenced the design of countless stadiums, arenas, and public spaces around the world. The use of tiered seating, arches, and vaulted ceilings—all features perfected by the Romans in the Colosseum—are now standard elements in the design of large public venues. Moreover, the Colosseum's emphasis on creating an immersive and inclusive spectator experience continues to resonate in the design of contemporary entertainment spaces.

The Colosseum's place in Roman architecture is not only defined by its scale and grandeur but by its lasting impact on architectural history. It represents the height of Roman engineering and design, a structure that embodies the values, ambitions, and innovations of an empire that sought to leave an indelible mark on the world. Today, the Colosseum stands as a monument to the ingenuity of Roman architects and engineers, a timeless symbol of Rome's architectural legacy that continues to inspire wonder and admiration centuries after its completion.

# Chapter 13: The Colosseum's Influence on Modern Stadiums

The influence of the Colosseum on modern stadiums is profound, shaping the way we design, build, and experience large public arenas today. Built nearly two thousand years ago, the Colosseum was a marvel of Roman engineering and architecture, setting a precedent for future structures with its innovative design, advanced construction techniques, and its focus on the needs of the spectators. While modern stadiums have incorporated advances in technology, materials, and comfort, many of the fundamental elements that define their design and function can be traced directly back to the Colosseum. From the architectural features to the way crowds are managed and the very purpose of these structures as centers of public entertainment, the Colosseum's legacy endures in today's largest sporting and concert venues.

One of the most obvious ways the Colosseum has influenced modern stadiums is through its overall architectural layout. The elliptical shape of the Colosseum, designed to maximize the number of spectators while providing optimal sightlines to the central arena, is mirrored in modern stadiums that aim to give attendees an unobstructed view of the action, whether it's a football match, a concert, or a track-and-field event. The elliptical or oval shape not only ensures that spectators are as close to the action as possible, regardless of their seating position, but also helps distribute the crowd evenly around the venue, facilitating better crowd control and movement.

The tiered seating arrangement of the Colosseum is another critical feature that has been carried over into modern stadium design. The Colosseum was designed with different levels of seating to accommodate the various social classes of Roman society. The wealthy elites and politicians sat closest to the arena on the lower levels, while the common citizens and women sat higher up. This separation of seating by status was an important feature in Roman times, reflecting the hierarchical nature of Roman society. While modern stadiums no longer segregate seating based on social status, the concept of tiered seating remains central. Today, stadiums feature multiple tiers or levels, with different sections offering varying levels of comfort and access, from premium seats close to the field to general admission seating higher up. This arrangement is designed to offer a range of options for different budgets while still ensuring that all spectators have a good view of the event. The ability to accommodate tens of thousands of people in such a well-organized fashion, while ensuring that every seat is functional and has a clear sightline to the central activity, is a direct inheritance from the design of the Colosseum.

The Colosseum's emphasis on accessibility and crowd management also laid the groundwork for modern stadium infrastructure. One of the most remarkable features of the Colosseum was its "vomitoria," or passageways, which allowed for efficient movement of large crowds in and out of the arena. These passageways, strategically placed throughout the structure, enabled spectators to exit the building quickly after events, avoiding congestion and ensuring safety. This system of entrances and exits was a significant innovation in Roman architecture and has been adopted by modern stadiums around the world. Today's stadiums feature multiple entrances and exits, often labeled with numbers or letters for easy navigation, just as the Colosseum had numbered arches. The concept of designing a venue with ease of access in mind, ensuring that crowds can enter and exit safely and quickly, is directly linked to the lessons learned from the Colosseum.

In addition to the practical aspects of crowd control, the Colosseum also pioneered the use of architectural features that enhanced the comfort and experience of spectators. For example, the Colosseum had an ingenious system of retractable awnings, known as the "velarium," which could be extended over the seating areas to provide shade on hot days. This attention to the comfort of the audience is a feature that modern stadiums have embraced, with many incorporating retractable roofs or shading systems to protect spectators from the elements. The idea of making the environment as pleasant as possible for attendees, whether through temperature control, shading, or protection from rain, is another legacy of the Colosseum's design. Modern stadiums like the Mercedes-Benz Stadium in Atlanta or the Millennium Stadium in Cardiff feature fully retractable roofs, allowing for games or events to be held in all weather conditions while keeping spectators comfortable, a concept that originated in ancient Rome.

Another significant influence of the Colosseum on modern stadiums is its use of multi-functional design. The Colosseum was not built solely for one type of event; it was a venue for a variety of public spectacles, including gladiatorial combats, animal hunts, public executions, and even large-scale mock naval battles. This versatility made the Colosseum a central hub of entertainment in ancient Rome, adaptable to a wide range of events. Modern stadiums have embraced this multi-functional approach, with venues being designed to host not only sporting events but also concerts, political rallies, and other large public gatherings. The ability to reconfigure the arena for different types of events, sometimes within a short time frame, is a direct descendant of the Colosseum's design, where the arena floor could be adapted for different types of spectacles, sometimes even being flooded to simulate naval battles.

Furthermore, the sheer scale of the Colosseum set a standard for large public venues that continues to inspire modern stadiums. With a seating capacity of over 50,000, the Colosseum was one of the largest structures of its kind in the ancient world. Today, many of the world's largest stadiums, such as Michigan Stadium in the United States or Rungrado 1st of May Stadium in North Korea, boast capacities well beyond 100,000, but they owe their conceptual design to the monumental ambition of the Colosseum. The desire to create venues that can accommodate vast numbers of people, while still maintaining structural integrity and aesthetic appeal, is a direct reflection of the architectural goals of the Colosseum's builders.

The Colosseum's use of concrete as a primary building material also set a precedent that has influenced modern stadium construction. Roman concrete, made from a mixture of volcanic ash, lime, and water, was an innovative material that allowed for the construction of massive structures like the Colosseum. The durability and flexibility of Roman concrete enabled the Colosseum to withstand the test of time, surviving earthquakes, fires, and the passage of centuries. Today, concrete remains one of the most commonly used materials in stadium construction due to its strength, versatility, and cost-effectiveness. Advances in modern concrete technology, including reinforced concrete, have allowed stadiums to be built on an even grander scale, but the essential properties of the material—its ability to support large structures while allowing for complex architectural designs—remain rooted in the innovations of Roman builders.

In terms of aesthetics, the Colosseum also influenced the design of modern stadiums through its grandeur and sense of spectacle. The exterior of the Colosseum, with its series of arches and columns, was designed to impress and awe both Romans and visitors to the city. This emphasis on creating a visually striking structure has carried over into modern stadium design, with many contemporary venues incorporating bold architectural features that make them landmarks in their own right. For example, the Allianz Arena in Munich is known for its distinctive illuminated facade, which can change colors depending on the event, while the Bird's Nest Stadium in Beijing, designed for the 2008 Olympic Games, has a unique lattice-like exterior that has made it an iconic structure. These modern stadiums, like the Colosseum, are not just functional spaces but symbols of civic pride and architectural innovation.

Additionally, the Colosseum's role as a social and political space has been mirrored in the way modern stadiums are used as venues for cultural expression and political events. In ancient Rome, the Colosseum was more than just a place for entertainment; it was a symbol of the emperor's power and a tool for maintaining public order. Emperors used the games to curry favor with the populace, demonstrate their generosity, and distract people from political issues. In a similar way, modern stadiums have become sites for important political and social moments, from the opening and closing ceremonies of the Olympic Games to concerts and rallies that draw tens of thousands of people. These events, like the spectacles in the Colosseum, serve to bring communities together, foster a sense of collective identity, and project the power and prestige of those who control the venues.

The legacy of the Colosseum's engineering and architectural brilliance is also evident in the increasing use of technology in modern stadiums. While the Colosseum relied on mechanical devices such as elevators and trapdoors to enhance the spectacle of the games, modern stadiums have taken this a step further with the integration of cutting-edge technology to enhance the fan experience. Massive video screens, state-of-the-art sound systems, retractable seating, and even artificial turf that can be moved in and out of the stadium are all features that can be seen as descendants of the technological innovations pioneered by the Romans. The concept of enhancing the viewer experience through technology, making events more immersive and dynamic, can be traced back to the Colosseum's efforts to create a multi-sensory spectacle for its audiences.

Finally, the cultural and symbolic significance of the Colosseum has been passed down to modern stadiums as well. In ancient Rome, the Colosseum was not just a venue for games; it was a representation of Roman power, engineering prowess, and the ability to bring people together. Similarly, modern stadiums have come to symbolize the cities and nations that build them. They are often seen as symbols of economic power, architectural innovation, and civic pride, just as the Colosseum was a symbol of the Roman Empire's might and grandeur.

In conclusion, the Colosseum's influence on modern stadiums is both profound and multifaceted, affecting nearly every aspect of stadium design and function, from architectural layout and crowd control to the integration of technology and the role of these venues in society. The legacy of the Colosseum lives on in the world's largest and most advanced arenas, demonstrating the lasting impact of Roman innovation on modern engineering and public architecture. Modern stadiums, like their ancient predecessor, continue to serve as centers of public entertainment and social gathering, reflecting the enduring human desire for spectacle, competition, and community.

# Chapter 14: The Daily Life of a Gladiator

The daily life of a gladiator in ancient Rome was a mixture of intense training, physical hardship, psychological pressure, and moments of fleeting glory. While the image of the gladiator has often been romanticized in popular culture, their reality was far more brutal, with lives dominated by the rigorous demands of survival, combat, and servitude. Gladiators were typically enslaved individuals, prisoners of war, criminals, or people who voluntarily sold themselves into the profession for the promise of money or fame, though they were often viewed as a lower class within Roman society. Despite the harshness of their existence, they played a critical role in Roman culture, becoming larger-than-life figures who entertained the masses with bloodsport in the grand arenas of Rome, most notably the Colosseum.

The day for a gladiator would typically begin early, often before dawn, in the gladiator schools known as *ludi*. These schools were where gladiators lived, trained, ate, and slept, and they were highly organized, militaristic environments. Upon waking, a gladiator would start their day with a meal. Their diet was highly regimented and surprisingly healthier than one might expect, as it needed to support the intense physical demands of their training and combat. Gladiators were sometimes referred to as "barley men" because their diet was heavy in carbohydrates, particularly from barley, grains, and legumes. Contrary to modern perceptions of athletes consuming large amounts of meat for protein, gladiators had a more plant-based diet. This high-carbohydrate intake helped them build a layer of body fat, which served as protection in combat. Though a lean, muscular physique might seem ideal for a fighter, the added fat provided some cushioning against cuts and blows, which could extend their survival during combat.

After eating, the next phase of their day involved rigorous physical training under the supervision of a *lanista*, the master of the gladiatorial school. The *lanista* was responsible for training gladiators and preparing them for the games. Training was relentless, and it focused not only on building physical strength but also on mastering the skills necessary to fight in the arena. Depending on their gladiator type—such as *murmillo*, *thraex*, *retiarius*, or *secutor*—they would be taught to use specific weapons and armor. For example, a *retiarius* fought with a net and a trident, relying on speed and agility, while a *murmillo* wielded a short sword and shield, requiring a different set of combat tactics focused on brute force and defense. Gladiators would spar with wooden swords called *rudis* before progressing to real weapons, allowing them to hone their skills without the risk of death during training.

The training was both physical and mental, designed to develop the endurance necessary to fight under extreme pressure in front of massive crowds. Gladiators were subjected to intense physical conditioning exercises, such as running, wrestling, and weightlifting, to build strength, stamina, and agility. They would also practice specific fighting techniques and strategies, often engaging in mock battles with other gladiators to simulate the conditions they would face in the arena. These mock battles could be as dangerous as the real thing, but they were critical for honing a gladiator's reflexes and combat instincts. The *lanista* would push them to their limits, using the threat of punishment or starvation as a motivator, as the survival of the gladiators depended on their ability to fight well and please the crowds.

A significant part of a gladiator's life was learning to cope with fear and death, as every fight could be their last. While some gladiators achieved fame and popularity, even becoming symbols of strength and courage to the Roman people, the reality was that they lived under the constant threat of injury or death. They were trained to fight in a way that would entertain the crowds, which meant their movements and tactics had to be not only effective but also dramatic and theatrical. Spectators wanted a good show, and that often meant fights were staged with an element of spectacle, including dramatic finishes where gladiators would have to either kill or be killed. The *lanista* would instill in them a mindset that prioritized honor in combat, teaching them to die well if it came to that, as a cowardly or ungraceful death would bring shame upon themselves and their school.

Despite the brutality of their existence, gladiators were not entirely isolated from the rest of Roman society. In fact, some gladiators attained a level of celebrity status, particularly those who managed to survive numerous bouts and earn victories in the arena. These successful gladiators could become folk heroes, their names and exploits being well-known across Rome. Gladiators like Spartacus, who famously led a rebellion, and others who became symbols of defiance or strength were admired, even if they were not fully accepted as equals in society. Those who were victorious in the arena might receive gifts from wealthy patrons, money, or even the coveted wooden sword, *rudis*, which symbolized their freedom. However, the possibility of fame was a double-edged sword. While it could lead to a degree of autonomy or even wealth, it also came with higher expectations, and more dangerous fights as their fame grew.

One of the psychological pressures that gladiators faced was the knowledge that, no matter how skilled they were, their fate was often decided by the whims of the crowd or the emperor. After each fight, a defeated gladiator's life was in the hands of the spectators and the presiding authority. The emperor or the crowd would signal with a thumbs-up or thumbs-down gesture to indicate whether the defeated gladiator should be spared or killed. The outcome depended as much on the crowd's mood or the gladiator's performance in the arena as on their combat ability. This uncertainty made every fight a gamble with life or death, adding to the psychological toll on gladiators. The pressure to not only survive but to entertain and earn the crowd's favor made their lives a constant balancing act between physical endurance and mental toughness.

Beyond the fighting itself, gladiators had to endure grueling living conditions. While gladiator schools provided food, shelter, and medical care, these amenities were often minimal, and life in the *ludi* was harsh. Gladiators were kept in small, cramped quarters, often chained when they weren't training or fighting. Their relationships with their fellow gladiators were complex; while they trained and lived together, they could also be forced to fight one another to the death in the arena. Friendships and alliances were fragile, as loyalty to each other had to be balanced with the need for individual survival. Some gladiators formed close bonds, particularly those who fought in the same style or came from similar backgrounds, but the knowledge that any one of them could be pitted against the other in the future created an underlying tension.

The medical care available to gladiators was one of the few advantages of their position, as owners of gladiator schools had a vested interest in keeping their fighters alive and healthy. Gladiators who survived battles with injuries were treated by specialized doctors, known as *medici*, who had experience treating wounds from combat. These doctors became skilled at stitching up cuts, setting broken bones, and dealing with the various injuries sustained in the arena. Gladiators who healed well enough could return to fight again, though repeated injuries often took a toll on their long-term health. While some gladiators succumbed to their injuries, others were able to recover and continue fighting, sometimes for years, until their bodies could no longer endure the punishment.

The hope of eventual freedom was a tantalizing dream for many gladiators, though it was a goal few would achieve. A gladiator who fought exceptionally well might be granted freedom, often symbolized by the presentation of the *rudis*. With freedom, a gladiator could leave the arena and try to reintegrate into society, though the stigma of their past often followed them. For those who were freed, some chose to become trainers or *lanistae* themselves, using their skills to train new generations of gladiators, while others attempted to return to normal civilian life. However, the path to freedom was narrow, and most gladiators lived short, brutal lives, dying in the arena or from injuries sustained in battle.

Despite the hardships, there were gladiators who found a sense of identity and purpose in their profession. For many, the gladiatorial life was not just about survival, but about mastering their skills, earning respect, and, for a select few, gaining fame. Some gladiators were able to earn their own small following among the public, and even though they were viewed as part of the lowest rungs of society, they could attain a level of admiration and fame that made their brutal existence worthwhile. The crowd's favor, the possibility of winning a fight and surviving to see another day, and the rare chance at freedom kept gladiators fighting, despite the ever-present danger.

In conclusion, the daily life of a gladiator was a grueling existence shaped by constant training, the threat of violence, and the hope for survival. While they were often viewed as little more than expendable fighters by Roman society, gladiators played a significant role in the culture and entertainment of the time. Their lives were defined by a unique combination of physical endurance, mental fortitude, and the need to please the crowd, making them both tragic and heroic figures in the history of ancient Rome. The legacy of the gladiators lives on, not only in the stories of their battles but in the enduring fascination with their lives, struggles, and the brutal world of the Roman arena.

# Chapter 15: The Art and Symbols of the Colosseum

The Colosseum, one of the most iconic structures in human history, is not only an architectural and engineering marvel but also a rich canvas of art and symbolism that reflected the culture, values, and politics of ancient Rome. Built between AD 70 and 80, the Colosseum was much more than a grand arena for gladiatorial games and public spectacles; it was a powerful statement of the Roman Empire's might and grandeur. The art and symbols that adorned the Colosseum, both in its original form and in the ways it was used, served as expressions of imperial authority, religious beliefs, and the social order of Roman life. Its elaborate designs and imagery made it a monumental space where the visual and symbolic representations of Roman power were as important as the spectacles that unfolded within its walls.

The Colosseum's exterior design is the first place to begin appreciating the art and symbolism that was built into this colossal amphitheater. Its facade was a stunning example of Roman architectural prowess, with three stories of arcades topped by a fourth story adorned with Corinthian pilasters and large rectangular windows. Each of the three lower stories featured different architectural orders: the first floor used the sturdy Doric order, the second floor the more graceful Ionic order, and the third the ornate Corinthian order. This progression from simplicity to complexity was not merely an artistic choice but a reflection of the Roman understanding of hierarchy and order. The different columns represented the structured and tiered nature of Roman society itself, with the simplest, strongest style at the base, representing the foundational classes, and the more decorative and refined styles above, symbolizing the elite. The arrangement mirrored the class stratification of Roman society, in which every individual had a place, from the slaves and commoners who sat in the upper tiers of the Colosseum to the aristocrats and emperors who occupied the most privileged seats closest to the action.

Carved into the arches and walls of the Colosseum were various reliefs and friezes that depicted scenes of Roman life and mythology. Many of these carvings have been lost over the centuries, but some evidence of their artistry remains. For example, it is believed that some of the arches were adorned with representations of Roman gods and goddesses, particularly deities associated with war and victory, such as Mars, the god of war, and Victoria, the goddess of victory. These figures would have loomed over the spectators, constantly reminding them of the divine forces that guided Roman conquests and the glory of the empire's military achievements. The inclusion of these gods in the very structure of the Colosseum underscored the idea that the games and spectacles held within were more than just entertainment—they were rituals that reaffirmed the might of Rome and its divinely sanctioned power.

The Colosseum also featured numerous statues that lined the upper levels of the structure. These statues, though now long gone, would have included depictions of Roman emperors, military leaders, and gods. The emperors, in particular, were a critical symbol of Roman authority and were often shown in poses that conveyed their role as protectors and rulers of the Roman people. These statues served as a constant reminder of the emperor's omnipresence and his connection to both the earthly and divine realms. As spectators entered the Colosseum, they would have passed beneath these towering figures, reinforcing the idea that they were under the watchful gaze of both the emperor and the gods.

In addition to its physical artwork, the Colosseum was a symbolic space where the empire's power and the subjugation of its enemies were on full display. This was most evident in the spectacles that took place within the arena, which often had profound symbolic meaning.

Gladiatorial games, for instance, were not only about violence and bloodshed but were also a form of political theater. The presence of the emperor and other elites at these games symbolized the central authority of the Roman state, while the battles between gladiators—many of whom were prisoners of war or enslaved individuals—represented the subjugation of Rome's enemies. The spectacle of combat between these warriors was a powerful visual metaphor for Rome's military dominance. Similarly, the venationes, or wild animal hunts, which were staged in the Colosseum, symbolized the taming of nature and the expansion of the empire into the wild, untamed territories of the world. Exotic animals from Africa, the Middle East, and Asia were brought to the arena, where they were hunted down in elaborate displays of Roman control over nature and distant lands.

The use of art and symbols extended beyond the arena floor and into the seating arrangement itself. The Colosseum was a highly stratified space, with seating that was carefully organized according to social rank. The emperor and his retinue occupied the best seats, known as the *podium*, which were closest to the action and provided the best views of the spectacles. Senators, magistrates, and members of the equestrian class were seated in the next tiers, followed by the common citizens and then, at the very top, the slaves and women. This strict division of seating reinforced the social hierarchy of Rome, and the very act of attending the games became a symbolic expression of one's place in the societal order. The architecture of the Colosseum thus served as a physical representation of the structure of Roman society, where each individual had a clearly defined role and status.

Another fascinating aspect of the Colosseum's symbolism was its association with imperial power and public generosity. The construction of the Colosseum was funded by the spoils of the Jewish War, including the looting of Jerusalem's Second Temple. This connection between military conquest and monumental construction was a key theme in Roman art and architecture, as emperors sought to demonstrate their strength and legitimacy through grand building projects. By using the wealth from their conquests to build public spaces like the Colosseum, emperors like Vespasian and Titus positioned themselves as benefactors of the Roman people, reinforcing the idea that their rule brought prosperity and grandeur to the empire. The Colosseum was a gift to the people, a place where they could witness the spectacles of the arena free of charge, and in this way, it served as a symbol of the emperor's generosity and care for his subjects.

The Colosseum also had a significant religious dimension, particularly in the early years of its operation. Public spectacles in Rome were often tied to religious festivals, and the games held in the Colosseum were no exception. Gladiatorial games, in particular, were originally linked to funerary rites and were thought to honor the spirits of the dead. As the games became more popular and institutionalized, they lost much of their religious significance, but the association between the arena and the divine remained. The games were still seen as offerings to the gods, particularly the gods of war and the underworld, and the arena became a space where the boundary between life and death was constantly negotiated.

Over the centuries, the Colosseum's symbols evolved as the empire changed. After the fall of the Roman Empire, the Colosseum became a site of Christian reverence. According to some accounts, early Christian martyrs were killed in the arena, though historical evidence for this is scarce. Nonetheless, the Colosseum became a potent symbol for the Christian church, representing the persecution of early Christians and their triumph over pagan Rome. By the medieval period, the Colosseum had come to symbolize the endurance of the Christian faith in the face of adversity, and it was even used as a place for Christian worship. The cross that stands in the Colosseum today serves as a reminder of this transformation and the layered history of the site.

In more modern times, the Colosseum has taken on new symbolic meanings. It has become a symbol of Rome itself and of the endurance of ancient Roman civilization. It is one of the most visited tourist attractions in the world, drawing millions of people each year who come to marvel at its scale, history, and significance. In this way, the Colosseum has transcended its original function as a venue for public spectacles and has become a global symbol of cultural heritage. It stands not only as a reminder of the power and grandeur of the Roman Empire but also as a testament to the enduring human fascination with history, architecture, and art.

In conclusion, the Colosseum's art and symbols were deeply intertwined with the political, social, and religious life of ancient Rome. From the statues and reliefs that adorned its exterior to the spectacles that took place within, the Colosseum was a space where the visual and symbolic representation of power was paramount. It was a place where the might of the empire was on display, where the hierarchy of Roman society was reinforced, and where the relationship between the people, the emperor, and the gods was constantly negotiated. Over the centuries, the symbolism of the Colosseum has evolved, but it remains a powerful reminder of the art, culture, and history of ancient Rome.

# Chapter 16: The Colosseum and the Fall of Rome

The Colosseum stands as a monumental testament to the glory of ancient Rome, but it also serves as a poignant reminder of the city's eventual decline and the fall of the Roman Empire. Constructed at the height of Roman power, the Colosseum symbolized the might, wealth, and engineering prowess of the empire, but as the centuries passed, it became a witness to Rome's gradual decay and the empire's eventual collapse. The relationship between the Colosseum and the fall of Rome is one of complex symbolism, historical events, and transformations that mirror the empire's shift from dominance to vulnerability.

When the Colosseum, also known as the Flavian Amphitheater, was completed in AD 80 under the reign of Emperor Titus, Rome was at the pinnacle of its power. The amphitheater was an architectural marvel, capable of seating between 50,000 to 80,000 spectators. Its construction was funded in large part by the spoils of the Jewish War, particularly the sacking of Jerusalem in AD 70. This connection between military conquest and public works was characteristic of the Roman Empire's might, using the wealth gained from its vast territories to fund grand monuments for the Roman people. The Colosseum was more than a place for entertainment; it was a symbol of Roman authority and imperial beneficence. The emperors used it to curry favor with the masses by hosting lavish spectacles such as gladiatorial games, beast hunts, and even mock naval battles. These events served not only to entertain but also to demonstrate the emperor's control over life and death, nature, and human conflict.

Yet, as the Colosseum rose to symbolize the might of Rome, the seeds of the empire's decline were already being sown. The reign of the Flavian emperors—Vespasian, Titus, and Domitian—marked a period of relative stability following the chaos of Nero's rule and the Year of the Four Emperors. However, beneath this apparent stability, Rome was grappling with the strains of overextension, economic inequality, and internal corruption. The lavish games held in the Colosseum were a form of "bread and circuses," designed to distract the populace from the deeper problems plaguing the empire. The emperor and ruling elites understood that the Colosseum could serve as a tool to pacify the masses, providing them with spectacles that showcased Rome's supposed invincibility and splendor. However, this outward show of strength could not conceal the cracks forming within the foundations of Roman society.

As the centuries passed, the Colosseum continued to be a vital part of Roman life, but its role began to change as the empire itself underwent significant transformations. By the time of the third century, Rome was in a state of crisis. The empire's borders were under constant pressure from barbarian invasions, and internal strife weakened the central authority. The Colosseum, which once hosted grand spectacles that celebrated the might of the Roman military, began to lose its significance as the empire struggled to maintain its territorial integrity and military power. The games and public spectacles became less frequent, and the Colosseum, like much of Rome's infrastructure, began to suffer from neglect.

The Crisis of the Third Century, which spanned from AD 235 to AD 284, was a period of near-collapse for the Roman Empire. The empire was divided by civil wars, economic collapse, plagues, and invasions from outside forces like the Goths and Vandals. During this time, the Colosseum's role in Roman society diminished. The financial strain on the empire meant fewer resources were available for public games and spectacles, and the building itself started to show signs of deterioration. Earthquakes and fires damaged parts of the structure, and the emperors who followed were more concerned with military defense than maintaining the grand arenas of the past. The Colosseum, once a symbol of Roman strength, began to reflect the weakening of the empire as a whole.

In AD 410, the city of Rome experienced a cataclysmic event that further marked the Colosseum's association with the fall of the empire. The Visigoths, led by King Alaric, sacked Rome for the first time in over 800 years. The shock of this invasion reverberated throughout the empire, signaling that Rome was no longer invincible. Though the Colosseum itself was not the primary target of the Visigoths, the symbolic weight of this event was immense. The sacking of Rome showed that the heart of the Roman Empire could be breached, and the Colosseum, as a symbol of the empire's grandeur, stood in stark contrast to the vulnerability of the city itself. The fact that the Colosseum remained standing even as the city was ravaged speaks to its enduring presence, but it also underscored the deepening decline of Rome's influence.

As the Western Roman Empire continued its downward spiral in the fifth century, the Colosseum saw less and less use. The games that had once thrilled Roman citizens became increasingly rare, both because of the economic costs and the shifting values of the empire's rulers. By this time, Christianity had become the dominant religion in the empire, and the association of the Colosseum with pagan spectacles, such as gladiatorial games and sacrifices, was increasingly at odds with Christian sensibilities. The games were officially banned by Emperor Honorius in AD 404, marking the end of an era. While some events, like venationes (animal hunts), continued for a few more decades, the Colosseum's role as the center of public entertainment had effectively come to an end.

The final blow to the Colosseum's role in Roman society came with the fall of the Western Roman Empire in AD 476. The last Roman emperor, Romulus Augustulus, was deposed by the barbarian king Odoacer, signaling the collapse of imperial authority in the West. In the centuries that followed, the Colosseum fell into disuse, and its fate mirrored that of the empire itself. The once-grand structure was subject to neglect, looting, and repurposing. Much of its stone was taken for other building projects, including churches and fortifications. The Colosseum's marble facade was stripped away, its iron clamps removed, and it became a quarry for materials rather than a symbol of Rome's might.

Despite its decline, the Colosseum remained an enduring symbol of the fallen empire. In the medieval period, it was used for various purposes, from housing to workshops, and even as a fortress. During the Renaissance, it became a popular subject for artists and scholars who sought to reconnect with Rome's ancient past. The building, though damaged and repurposed, never lost its association with the grandeur of the Roman Empire. In many ways, the Colosseum came to symbolize both the glory of Rome and the fragility of even the most powerful civilizations.

In modern times, the Colosseum has been restored and preserved as a UNESCO World Heritage Site, and it stands as one of the most visited landmarks in the world. Yet, its historical association with the fall of Rome remains a central part of its story. The Colosseum reminds us that even the most powerful empires are subject to the forces of time, change, and decline. Its massive structure, still standing after nearly two thousand years, is a testament to the skill and vision of Roman architects and engineers, but it also serves as a symbol of how the empire that built it eventually fell into ruin.

The Colosseum's journey from the center of Roman life to a relic of a fallen empire is emblematic of Rome's own trajectory. In its heyday, it was a place where the power and majesty of the empire were displayed in the most spectacular and brutal ways. It was a space where emperors demonstrated their control over both nature and humanity, where the people of Rome gathered to witness spectacles that celebrated the empire's conquests and dominance. But as Rome's fortunes waned, the Colosseum too fell into decline, its once-glorious halls echoing with the silence of a civilization that had lost its way. Today, as we walk through its ancient corridors and gaze upon its crumbling arches, we are reminded not only of Rome's grandeur but also of the impermanence of even the greatest empires. The Colosseum and the fall of Rome are intertwined in history, each telling the story of the other in stone and silence.

# Chapter 17: Earthquakes and the Colosseum's Ruins

The Colosseum, one of the most iconic landmarks of ancient Rome, has endured the ravages of time, war, and natural disasters. Among the most significant events that have contributed to the damage and degradation of this colossal structure are the many earthquakes that struck Rome over the centuries. Earthquakes played a pivotal role in transforming the once-majestic amphitheater into the ruins that stand today, a shadow of its former glory. These seismic events were not just destructive forces, but catalysts for change, shifting the way the Colosseum was used, viewed, and even repurposed throughout history.

The construction of the Colosseum began in AD 72 under Emperor Vespasian and was completed in AD 80 by his son Titus. It was a marvel of Roman engineering and architecture, a testament to the skill of Roman builders who designed it to host a variety of grand spectacles, including gladiatorial combat, public executions, and animal hunts. Its elliptical shape, towering arches, and advanced systems for crowd management and stagecraft made it the largest amphitheater ever built. However, despite its grandeur and engineering sophistication, the Colosseum could not withstand the natural forces that would soon begin to test its resilience.

Rome has historically been subject to seismic activity due to its proximity to tectonic fault lines. Earthquakes have been recorded throughout the history of the region, and the Colosseum, being a massive stone structure, was particularly vulnerable to their tremors. Over the centuries, these earthquakes caused significant damage to the amphitheater, leading to its gradual decline and eventual transformation into the ruin we see today.

The first recorded major earthquake to affect the Colosseum occurred in AD 217, during the reign of Emperor Macrinus. While detailed accounts of the event are scarce, it is known that the earthquake caused significant damage to the upper levels of the amphitheater. The roof and some of the seating sections were damaged, necessitating repairs. It took several years before the Colosseum was fully restored and reopened for public use. During this time, the games were temporarily moved to other venues in Rome. Although the repairs allowed the Colosseum to continue functioning as the centerpiece of Roman entertainment, the earthquake marked the beginning of a series of natural disasters that would slowly erode the stability and integrity of the structure.

Another significant earthquake struck Rome in AD 443, during the declining years of the Western Roman Empire. By this time, the empire was facing immense political, military, and economic challenges, and the Colosseum had already seen a reduction in its use for public games. The earthquake caused considerable damage to the amphitheater, particularly to the southern side of the structure, where sections of the outer wall collapsed. This event marked a turning point in the Colosseum's history, as the resources needed for repairs were increasingly scarce, and the Roman Empire was in no position to invest in the restoration of its once-great monuments.

As the Western Roman Empire fell in AD 476, the Colosseum entered a period of neglect and deterioration. With the decline of imperial power, the maintenance of large public buildings like the Colosseum became less of a priority. The amphitheater was still occasionally used for smaller-scale events, but its days as the grand stage of Roman spectacle were over. The city of Rome itself was subject to further seismic activity, and the Colosseum continued to suffer from the effects of earthquakes.

One of the most catastrophic earthquakes to hit Rome and damage the Colosseum occurred in the year 801, during the reign of Charlemagne, who had been crowned Holy Roman Emperor just a year earlier. This earthquake caused massive structural damage to the

Colosseum, with large sections of the outer walls collapsing and much of the remaining upper structure becoming unstable. The southern side of the amphitheater, which had already been weakened by previous quakes, suffered the most damage. This event left the Colosseum in a state of partial ruin, and it was never fully repaired. Over the following centuries, the collapsed sections of the structure were left as they were, and the once-magnificent arena began to take on the appearance of a ruin.

The damage caused by earthquakes was not just limited to the physical structure of the Colosseum; it also had a profound effect on how the building was perceived and used. As the city of Rome transitioned from the capital of a vast empire to a medieval city-state, the Colosseum's role in society changed. The building, once a symbol of imperial grandeur, became a source of building materials for other construction projects in Rome. Stones, bricks, and even metal from the Colosseum were scavenged and repurposed for new buildings, churches, and fortifications. This process, known as spoliation, was common in the medieval period as people sought to reuse materials from ancient Roman buildings. The earthquakes had already weakened the Colosseum, and the removal of its materials only hastened its decay.

One of the most significant earthquakes in the Colosseum's history occurred in 1349. This earthquake, one of the largest ever recorded in Rome, caused the southern side of the Colosseum to collapse almost entirely. The massive blocks of travertine stone that formed the outer wall tumbled down, leaving a gaping hole in the structure that is still visible today. The collapse of the southern wall exposed the interior of the Colosseum to the elements, accelerating its deterioration. The earthquake of 1349 was a defining moment in the Colosseum's transformation from a functional building to a ruin, and it marked the end of any serious attempts to restore the structure for public use.

In the centuries following the 1349 earthquake, the Colosseum was further repurposed for various uses. It was used as a quarry for building materials, as a fortress by Roman noble families, and even as a Christian shrine. The damage caused by the earthquakes had left the structure unstable, and much of the interior seating and stage areas were lost. However, despite its ruined state, the Colosseum retained a powerful symbolic presence in the city. By the Renaissance, it had become a popular subject for artists and scholars who sought to preserve the memory of ancient Rome's architectural achievements.

The earthquakes that struck the Colosseum also played a role in shaping its modern legacy. The ruins of the Colosseum, with their broken arches and crumbling walls, became a symbol of the impermanence of human achievement. The sight of the once-mighty amphitheater in ruins inspired generations of poets, writers, and artists. The Colosseum's ruined state also became a symbol of the fall of the Roman Empire itself, a reminder that even the most powerful civilizations are vulnerable to the forces of nature and time.

In the 18th and 19th centuries, efforts were made to stabilize the Colosseum and preserve what remained of the structure. Engineers and architects worked to reinforce the surviving walls and prevent further collapse. While these efforts have helped to protect the Colosseum from additional damage, the marks of the earthquakes are still clearly visible today. The southern side of the amphitheater remains partially collapsed, and the irregular shape of the building is a testament to the seismic forces that have shaped its history.

Today, the Colosseum stands as both a ruin and a monument to ancient Roman engineering and architectural ingenuity. The damage caused by earthquakes over the centuries is an integral part of its story, a reminder of the powerful natural forces that have shaped the landscape of Rome and the fortunes of its most famous landmarks. The Colosseum's ability to endure despite the devastation of earthquakes speaks to the strength of its original design, but it also underscores the fragility of even the most magnificent human creations. The earthquakes that damaged the Colosseum may have reduced it to a shadow of its former self, but they also helped to transform it into one of the most iconic and enduring symbols of Rome's ancient past.

In the modern era, seismic activity in Rome is closely monitored, and efforts continue to preserve and protect the Colosseum from further damage. Conservation efforts have ensured that the remaining structure is stable, but the risk of earthquakes remains ever-present. The Colosseum's long history of surviving earthquakes is a testament to the enduring legacy of Roman engineering, as well as a reminder of the power of nature to shape human history. As visitors walk through the ruins today, they are not only witnessing the grandeur of ancient Rome but also the lasting impact of the earthquakes that have left their indelible mark on one of the world's greatest architectural achievements.

# Chapter 18: The Preservation of the Colosseum Today

The Colosseum, a monumental testament to ancient Roman engineering and architectural prowess, has stood for nearly two thousand years, surviving wars, earthquakes, and the passage of time. Today, its preservation has become a priority, not only because of its historical significance but also due to its cultural, architectural, and symbolic importance in representing the grandeur of the Roman Empire. The preservation of the Colosseum is a complex and multifaceted endeavor that involves a blend of historical research, cutting-edge technology, engineering innovation, and global cooperation. Ensuring that this ancient structure endures for future generations is no easy task. Every crack, every stone, and every feature of the amphitheater presents unique challenges that modern preservationists must address with care, precision, and reverence for its ancient heritage.

Preserving the Colosseum today involves a careful balance between conserving its remaining structure and making it accessible to millions of visitors who flock to Rome each year. At the heart of these efforts is a commitment to maintaining the integrity of the amphitheater while also adapting to the needs of the modern world. Rome's city authorities, Italian conservation agencies, and international bodies such as UNESCO all play vital roles in the preservation process. Since the Colosseum was designated a UNESCO World Heritage Site in 1980, it has been protected as a site of international importance. However, safeguarding it from natural deterioration, environmental factors, and the impact of tourism requires ongoing attention and effort.

The process of preserving the Colosseum can be traced back several centuries. The building first gained attention from Renaissance artists, architects, and scholars, who recognized its historical value and sought to protect it from further decay. During the Renaissance, early preservationists began to advocate for the protection of Rome's ancient ruins, and the Colosseum became a focal point of these efforts. However, the most significant modern attempts at preservation began in the 19th and 20th centuries when extensive damage caused by natural disasters and human activity demanded that something be done to stabilize the structure. Many parts of the building had been scavenged for materials, and earthquakes had caused severe damage, particularly to the southern side of the Colosseum, leaving it vulnerable to further collapse.

One of the major projects of the modern era was undertaken in the 1800s under the Papal government, which initiated the first large-scale efforts to protect the Colosseum from further deterioration. During this period, architects and engineers focused on reinforcing the surviving walls, which had been weakened by centuries of damage. Large metal supports and buttresses were added to stabilize the structure, particularly around the collapsed portions of the outer wall. These early efforts laid the groundwork for future preservation projects, marking the beginning of a long-term commitment to safeguarding the Colosseum for future generations.

In the 20th century, with the rise of modern conservation techniques and scientific methods, the preservation of the Colosseum entered a new phase. A landmark project was launched in the 1930s under Mussolini's regime, which sought to restore parts of the Colosseum as a symbol of Italy's Roman heritage. However, these early restoration efforts were not without controversy. Some scholars and conservationists criticized the use of modern materials and methods, arguing that they were not in keeping with the historical authenticity of the site. Nonetheless, these efforts helped to stabilize the structure and brought international attention to the importance of preserving Rome's ancient monuments.

The Colosseum's preservation entered a new era in the late 20th and early 21st centuries, as more advanced technologies and conservation methodologies became available. Modern preservation efforts are guided by a philosophy that seeks to balance historical integrity with the need for intervention. Instead of focusing solely on restoring the amphitheater to its former state, modern conservators prioritize stabilization and protection, ensuring that the structure can stand safely without altering its historical fabric. This approach involves constant monitoring and maintenance, as the Colosseum faces a variety of environmental and human-induced threats that could lead to further deterioration if not carefully managed.

One of the most pressing challenges facing the Colosseum today is environmental degradation. Over the centuries, the amphitheater has been exposed to a variety of harmful environmental factors, including pollution, acid rain, and seismic activity. The Colosseum's stone façade is particularly vulnerable to these elements, and the impact of pollution has caused significant wear and erosion on the ancient stones. In recent decades, as Rome's air quality has worsened due to increased industrial activity and automobile traffic, the Colosseum has faced greater threats from air pollution. The stone surfaces, particularly the travertine and tuff, have been affected by the deposition of particulate matter and corrosive pollutants, leading to surface erosion and blackening.

To combat these issues, modern preservationists employ a range of advanced techniques to clean and protect the Colosseum's surfaces. One of the most widely used methods is laser cleaning, which allows conservators to remove pollutants and dirt from the stone without damaging the underlying material. This technique has proven to be highly effective in restoring the Colosseum's original color and protecting it from further environmental damage. Additionally, protective coatings are often applied to the stone surfaces to shield them from the harmful effects of pollution and weathering.

Another significant threat to the Colosseum comes from seismic activity. Rome, located near several fault lines, is prone to earthquakes, and the Colosseum has been particularly vulnerable to these natural disasters. Over the centuries, several major earthquakes have caused extensive damage to the structure, leading to the collapse of sections of the outer wall and the weakening of its foundations. Today, seismic monitoring systems are in place to track any movements or shifts in the ground beneath the Colosseum, allowing for early detection of potential threats. Engineers and preservationists have also worked to reinforce the structure using modern materials and techniques that can withstand seismic forces. The use of modern reinforcement materials, such as steel supports and advanced adhesives, helps to stabilize the Colosseum's walls and arches without compromising the historical integrity of the building.

Tourism, while essential for raising awareness and funding preservation efforts, poses another challenge to the Colosseum's long-term survival. Millions of visitors flock to the Colosseum each year, and the constant foot traffic has a noticeable impact on the structure. The wear and tear caused by visitors, combined with the potential for accidental damage, necessitates careful management of tourist access. To address this issue, Italian authorities have implemented strict regulations on visitor access to certain parts of the Colosseum, limiting the number of people allowed inside at any given time. Additionally, designated pathways and protective barriers have been installed to prevent damage to sensitive areas of the amphitheater.

The funding and financial support required to preserve the Colosseum are significant. The Italian government, along with international organizations and private donors, plays a key role in financing preservation projects. One of the most notable contributions came in 2011, when the Italian luxury fashion brand Tod's pledged over €25 million to fund a comprehensive restoration of the Colosseum. This project, which included cleaning the façade, reinforcing the structure, and improving visitor access, marked one of the largest private investments in the preservation of a cultural heritage site in Italy. Such partnerships between the public and private sectors are crucial to ensuring the continued preservation of the Colosseum, as the costs associated with its maintenance are substantial.

Beyond physical preservation, there is also a growing emphasis on using modern technology to enhance our understanding of the Colosseum and its history. Digital tools such as 3D scanning, virtual reality (VR), and augmented reality (AR) have revolutionized the way researchers and visitors interact with the site. These technologies allow for detailed mapping of the Colosseum's structure, providing valuable data on its condition and helping conservators make informed decisions about preservation. Moreover, virtual reconstructions of the Colosseum offer visitors a glimpse into what the amphitheater might have looked like during its heyday, enhancing the educational experience without altering the physical site.

The future of the Colosseum's preservation lies not only in safeguarding its physical structure but also in fostering a deeper understanding of its cultural and historical significance. Educational programs, exhibitions, and scholarly research are integral components of the preservation effort. By promoting a greater appreciation for the Colosseum's history, these initiatives help ensure that future generations will continue to value and protect this ancient monument. Institutions such as Rome's Archaeological Superintendency and various universities around the world collaborate on research projects that shed new light on the Colosseum's construction, use, and cultural impact.

In conclusion, the preservation of the Colosseum today is a complex and ongoing effort that requires the collaboration of conservationists, engineers, architects, scientists, and historians. It involves not only physical restoration and protection but also the careful management of environmental, seismic, and human-induced threats. Modern technology, international cooperation, and financial support are all vital components of the preservation process. As one of the most recognizable symbols of ancient Rome, the Colosseum stands as a testament to human ingenuity, endurance, and the enduring legacy of Roman civilization. Through the diligent efforts of those committed to its preservation, this magnificent structure will continue to inspire and educate people for centuries to come.

# Chapter 19: The Colosseum as a Symbol of Rome

The Colosseum, towering in the heart of Rome, is more than just an ancient amphitheater—it stands as a profound symbol of the city itself, representing Rome's rich and turbulent history, its architectural ingenuity, and the cultural impact that continues to resonate through time. When people think of Rome, one of the first images that come to mind is the Colosseum, a structure that has come to embody the strength, grandeur, and resilience of the Roman Empire. This symbolism transcends the physical structure, delving deep into what the Colosseum represents on a cultural, political, and societal level. From its original purpose as a venue for gladiatorial combat and grand spectacles to its enduring status as a global icon of Rome, the Colosseum's meaning has evolved, yet it remains central to Rome's identity.

At its inception, the Colosseum was constructed under the Flavian emperors, Vespasian and his sons Titus and Domitian, as a powerful symbol of Roman might and imperial authority. The very decision to build such a grand structure was a deliberate political move by Vespasian to erase the dark legacy of Nero, whose self-indulgent rule had left the Roman populace disillusioned. Nero had previously constructed the lavish Domus Aurea, a personal palace on land devastated by the Great Fire of Rome. Vespasian, in stark contrast, returned this land to the people of Rome by building the Colosseum on its grounds. Thus, the Colosseum was born as a symbol of the new leadership's commitment to the Roman people, a gift that symbolized unity, strength, and prosperity under the Flavian dynasty. It was a reminder to all of the power and benevolence of the emperors, and of Rome's supremacy in the ancient world.

From the moment the Colosseum opened its doors in 80 AD, it became the epicenter of public life in Rome. Thousands of Romans, regardless of their social standing, would gather within its walls to witness grand spectacles. The structure itself was a reflection of Roman society—its seating arrangement divided by class, with the elite positioned closest to the arena and the lower classes relegated to the upper tiers. The games that took place in the Colosseum were a microcosm of the Roman Empire's power and dominance. Gladiatorial combat, animal hunts, and even mock sea battles showcased the might of Roman military prowess, while simultaneously offering the citizens of Rome an escape from the hardships of daily life. In this sense, the Colosseum was more than just a building; it was a social stage where the dynamics of Roman society played out before the public eye, reinforcing the hierarchical structure that underpinned the empire.

Yet, even as it served as a symbol of imperial power and public unity, the Colosseum also came to symbolize the complexities of Roman civilization itself. The brutal spectacles of bloodshed and death that took place within its arena reflect the darker aspects of Roman culture, where violence and entertainment were deeply intertwined. Gladiators, who often fought to the death for the amusement of the crowd, were both revered and reviled, serving as symbols of human endurance, strength, and the cruelty of Roman entertainment. For many, the Colosseum represents the contradictions of ancient Rome—a civilization that produced incredible feats of art, engineering, and governance, yet reveled in the spectacle of death and destruction.

As centuries passed and the Roman Empire declined, the Colosseum too began to fall into ruin. Following the fall of Rome in the 5th century, the Colosseum's original purpose as a venue for public games ceased, and the amphitheater fell victim to neglect and decay. However, rather than fading into obscurity, the Colosseum transformed into a symbol of Rome's resilience. Even in its ruined state, the Colosseum remained an iconic presence in the landscape of the Eternal City, a testament to the grandeur of Rome's past. The structure became a quarry for building materials during the Middle Ages, as stones from the Colosseum were repurposed to construct churches and other buildings throughout Rome. Despite this, the Colosseum's symbolic power only grew. It was a reminder of the enduring legacy of the Roman Empire, even as new civilizations rose and fell.

The Renaissance era saw a revival of interest in the Colosseum, as scholars, architects, and artists from across Europe flocked to Rome to study the ruins of the ancient city. The Colosseum, in particular, captured the imagination of Renaissance thinkers, who saw in its crumbling arches and broken walls a symbol of both the greatness and fragility of human achievement. Artists like Michelangelo and Raphael sketched the Colosseum, incorporating its majestic forms into their work and helping to cement its status as a symbol of Rome's artistic and architectural heritage. During this period, the Colosseum came to represent not only the glory of ancient Rome but also the potential for rebirth and renewal that defined the Renaissance itself.

In the centuries that followed, the Colosseum took on new layers of meaning as a symbol of Christian martyrdom. Although historical evidence suggests that the Colosseum was not a primary site for Christian executions, it became associated with the suffering of early Christians under Roman persecution. By the 18th century, the Colosseum was recognized as a sacred site, and Pope Benedict XIV consecrated the building as a Christian monument. This new religious symbolism added another dimension to the Colosseum's role as a symbol of Rome, linking it to the broader narrative of Christianity's rise from persecution to dominance within the Roman Empire. Pilgrims visiting Rome viewed the Colosseum as a place of reflection and reverence, a stark contrast to its earlier role as a venue for brutal entertainment.

In modern times, the Colosseum remains a powerful symbol of Rome and its history, but its meaning has expanded beyond the borders of Italy to become a global icon. As one of the most visited tourist attractions in the world, the Colosseum represents the enduring allure of ancient Rome and the fascination that the Roman Empire continues to hold over people from all walks of life. For many, the Colosseum is a symbol of the enduring nature of human civilization—proof that even the greatest empires leave behind lasting legacies that shape the world for millennia to come. The Colosseum stands not just as a relic of the past, but as a living symbol of Rome's ability to endure and adapt through the ages.

In recent years, the Colosseum has also taken on new meanings in response to contemporary events. It has become a site for protests, vigils, and public gatherings, symbolizing not only the power of Rome's history but also the continuing struggle for human rights and justice. For example, the Colosseum is lit up at night on various occasions to raise awareness for causes such as the abolition of the death penalty and the promotion of world peace. In these moments, the Colosseum becomes more than a historical monument—it serves as a platform for contemporary issues, a symbol of global solidarity, and a reminder that the lessons of history are still relevant in the modern world.

In conclusion, the Colosseum's role as a symbol of Rome is multi-faceted and ever-evolving. From its origins as a symbol of imperial power and public unity, to its transformation into a symbol of Christian martyrdom and artistic inspiration, to its present-day status as a global icon, the Colosseum continues to reflect the complexities of Rome's history and its place in the world. Its enduring presence in the heart of Rome serves as a constant reminder of the city's rich and tumultuous past, while its cultural significance reaches far beyond Italy's borders, touching the lives and imaginations of people across the globe. The Colosseum, in all its grandeur and ruin, is a symbol of the endurance of human achievement and the lasting legacy of Rome's impact on the world.

# Chapter 20: Legends and Myths of the Colosseum

The Colosseum, a monumental amphitheater standing proudly in the heart of ancient Rome, is not only a marvel of engineering and a symbol of the Roman Empire's power but also a wellspring of legends and myths that have been woven into its historical narrative. Over the centuries, the grand arena has inspired countless stories, some based on historical events, others emerging from the imaginations of those who stood in awe of its sheer grandeur. These legends and myths serve to enhance the mystique of the Colosseum, transforming it from a mere architectural structure into a timeless monument that stirs the human spirit.

One of the most enduring myths associated with the Colosseum is the story of Christian martyrdom. It is widely believed, particularly in popular culture, that thousands of early Christians were brutally killed in the Colosseum during the reign of various Roman emperors. These accounts paint a dramatic picture of Christians being thrown to lions or burned alive, suffering under the ruthless gaze of a bloodthirsty audience. This image has been perpetuated through countless retellings in literature, film, and religious teachings, making it one of the most iconic stories associated with the Colosseum. However, historians and archaeologists have found little evidence to support the notion that large-scale Christian executions took place within the Colosseum itself. While Christians were undoubtedly persecuted in ancient Rome, and some may have been killed in other arenas or public spectacles, the association between the Colosseum and Christian martyrdom seems to be more rooted in legend than in fact. Nevertheless, this myth has become so ingrained in the cultural and religious history of the Colosseum that, to this day, the amphitheater is seen by many as a sacred site of Christian suffering and sacrifice.

Another popular legend surrounding the Colosseum is the story of its subterranean labyrinth, a mysterious underground network of tunnels and chambers that has captivated the imaginations of visitors for centuries. This underground area, known as the hypogeum, was used to house gladiators, wild animals, and stage props, creating an elaborate system that allowed for the dramatic and sudden appearances of combatants and beasts during the games. Over time, the hypogeum became the subject of various myths, with some claiming that it was home to secret cults, underground rituals, or even treasure hidden by the Roman emperors. One persistent legend suggests that the hypogeum was connected to a vast underground city beneath Rome, where fugitives and outcasts could live in hiding, avoiding the gaze of imperial authorities. Though this legend is likely far-fetched, it speaks to the aura of mystery and danger that surrounded the Colosseum's underground chambers. Even today, as archaeologists continue to uncover more about the hypogeum, the fascination with its hidden depths persists, lending an air of intrigue to the already awe-inspiring structure above.

The Colosseum's association with wild animals is another source of myth. During its heyday, the arena hosted venationes, or animal hunts, where exotic beasts from all corners of the Roman Empire were brought to fight gladiators or each other for the entertainment of the crowd. Lions, tigers, bears, and even elephants were pitted against men in these gruesome spectacles. Over time, stories began to circulate about the sheer scale of these events, with some claiming that hundreds or even thousands of animals were killed in a single day. One particularly vivid myth describes how Emperor Titus, to celebrate the opening of the Colosseum, ordered 9,000 wild animals to be slaughtered during the inaugural games. While the number of animals killed during the games was undoubtedly high, the exact figures are likely exaggerated. These tales of mass carnage, while partially rooted in truth, have been embellished over time, contributing to the Colosseum's reputation as a place of unimaginable violence and death.

There are also legends that speak to the supernatural aspects of the Colosseum. Given its long history of bloodshed, it is no surprise that the amphitheater has become a focal point for ghost stories and tales of haunted apparitions. According to some accounts, the spirits of gladiators who perished in the arena still roam the Colosseum at night, their tortured souls unable to find peace after their violent deaths. Visitors and locals alike have reported eerie sensations when walking through the ancient structure after dark—cold drafts, disembodied whispers, and shadowy figures moving through the corridors. Some claim to have heard the roar of the crowd or the clash of swords echoing faintly through the ruins, as if the Colosseum itself is replaying the brutal spectacles of the past. These ghostly tales have added another layer of mystique to the Colosseum, making it a popular destination not only for history buffs but also for those interested in the paranormal.

Another fascinating myth surrounding the Colosseum involves the supposed role of Emperor Nero in its construction. As the story goes, the Colosseum was originally part of Nero's opulent palace complex, the Domus Aurea, which included an enormous artificial lake. After Nero's death, his successors sought to distance themselves from his tyrannical rule and ordered the lake to be drained and replaced with a public amphitheater for the enjoyment of the Roman people. The Colosseum, according to this legend, was built directly over the site of Nero's lake as a symbolic gesture to erase his legacy and restore the land to the citizens of Rome. While there is some truth to this story—Nero's extravagant palace did occupy the area where the Colosseum now stands—the narrative that the amphitheater was built specifically to erase Nero's memory is likely an oversimplification. Nonetheless, the legend persists, cementing the Colosseum's role not only as a venue for public entertainment but also as a monument to the triumph of the Roman people over the excesses of their emperors.

The mythic status of the Colosseum was further solidified during the Middle Ages, when the arena fell into disuse and began to crumble into ruin. As the structure decayed, it became the subject of apocalyptic prophecies and mystical interpretations. One famous legend, recorded by the Venerable Bede in the 8th century, proclaimed that "as long as the Colosseum stands, Rome shall stand; when the Colosseum falls, Rome shall fall; and when Rome falls, the world will end." This prophecy, though likely exaggerated, captured the imaginations of medieval Europeans, who viewed the Colosseum as a symbol of Rome's enduring power and influence. The idea that the fate of the world was somehow tied to the fate of the Colosseum gave the ancient structure an almost divine significance, transforming it into a monument not only of Roman civilization but of humanity itself. Even as the Colosseum lay in ruins, its mythic importance grew, and it became a pilgrimage site for those seeking to connect with the ancient past.

In modern times, the legends and myths of the Colosseum continue to captivate the public imagination. Films, books, and television shows often depict the Colosseum as a place of grand spectacle, brutal violence, and historical intrigue, drawing on both historical facts and the myths that have emerged over centuries. The image of gladiators fighting to the death in the Colosseum has become a symbol of ancient Rome's might and cruelty, while the legends of Christian martyrdom have imbued the structure with a sense of religious significance. The Colosseum, in this way, serves as a canvas onto which various stories and interpretations can be projected, each generation adding its own layer of meaning to the ancient monument.

In conclusion, the legends and myths of the Colosseum are as vast and varied as the structure itself. From tales of Christian martyrdom to ghostly apparitions, from underground labyrinths to mass animal slaughters, these stories have helped to shape the way we view the

Colosseum today. While many of these myths may not be grounded in historical fact, they contribute to the Colosseum's enduring mystique, transforming it from a mere relic of the past into a living monument that continues to inspire awe and wonder. The legends of the Colosseum remind us that history is not just about facts and dates—it is also about the stories we tell, the meanings we create, and the ways in which we connect with the past. Whether viewed as a symbol of imperial power, a sacred site of Christian suffering, or a haunted ruin filled with ghostly echoes, the Colosseum remains one of the most iconic and evocative monuments in the world, its legends and myths continuing to captivate the imaginations of people across the globe.

# Epilogue

As we reach the end of our journey through the Colosseum, it's clear that this ancient arena is much more than just a relic of the past. The Colosseum is a testament to the incredible achievements of the Roman Empire and a symbol of human ingenuity, courage, and ambition.

Over the centuries, the Colosseum has withstood earthquakes, wars, and the passage of time, yet it remains a powerful reminder of a world long gone. It tells the story of gladiators who fought bravely, of emperors who sought to entertain and impress their people, and of a society that valued both spectacle and strength.

Today, the Colosseum stands as one of the most famous landmarks in the world, drawing millions of visitors who come to marvel at its grandeur and imagine what life was like in Ancient Rome. It serves as a bridge between the past and the present, connecting us to a time when Rome ruled the known world.

But the story of the Colosseum isn't just about the past; it's also about the future. As we continue to study and preserve this magnificent structure, we ensure that future generations can learn from its history and be inspired by its legacy. The Colosseum reminds us that while time moves forward, the stories and lessons of the past will always have a place in our world.

As you close this book, remember that the Colosseum is more than just an arena—it's a symbol of endurance, of history, and of the human spirit. Whether you visit it in person or in your imagination, the Colosseum will always be a place where the echoes of ancient Rome can still be heard.

Thank you for joining this adventure through the Colosseum's storied past. The arena may be silent now, but its stories will live on forever.

The End.